W9-CCC-897

# THE
# ATLAS
## OF
# ANCIENT
# WORLDS

Written by Anne Millard
Illustrated by Russell Barnett

DORLING KINDERSLEY
LONDON • NEW YORK • STUTTGART

**A DORLING KINDERSLEY BOOK**

**Project Editor** Fran Jones
**Art Editor** Lester Cheeseman
**Production** Shelagh Gibson
**Managing Editor** Susan Peach
**Managing Art Editor** Jacquie Gulliver
**U.S. Editor** Chuck A. Wills

**History Consultants**

David Anderson, History Department,
School of Oriental and African Studies, University of London

Penny Bateman, Education Service, British Museum, London

Lucy Anne Bishop, The Horniman Museum, London

George Hart, Education Service, British Museum, London

Stephanie Haygarth, Australian Institute of Aboriginal and
Torres Strait Islander Studies, Canberra

Simon James, Education Service, British Museum, London

Professor Robert Layton, Department of Anthropology,
University of Durham

John Marr, Bhavan Institute of Indian Culture, London

Keith Nicklin, The Horniman Museum, London

Carl Phillips, Institute of Archaeology, London

Jane Portall, Department of Oriental Antiquities,
British Museum, London

Jill Varndell, Education Service, British Museum, London

First American Edition, 1994
2 4 6 8 10 9 7 5 3

Published in the United States by
Dorling Kindersley, Inc., 232 Madison Avenue
New York, New York 10016

Copyright © 1994 Dorling Kindersley Limited, London

All rights reserved under International and Pan-American Copyright
Conventions. No part of this publication may be reproduced, stored in
a retrieval system, or transmitted in any form or by any means, electronic,
mechanical, photocopying, recording, or otherwise, without the prior
written permission of the copyright owner. Published in Great Britain
by Dorling Kindersley Limited.

**Library of Congress Cataloging-in-Publication Data**
The Atlas of ancient worlds. — 1st American ed.
　　p.　cm.
　　Includes index.
　　ISBN 1-56458-471-2
　　1. Civilization, Ancient—Juvenile literature. 2. Civilization,
Ancient—Maps—Juvenile literature. [1. Civilization, Ancient.
2. Atlases.] I. Dorling Kindersley, Inc.
CB311.A85 1994
930—dc20　　　　　　　　　　　93-27041
　　　　　　　　　　　　　　　　　CIP
　　　　　　　　　　　　　　　　　AC

Reproduced in Singapore by
Koford International Private Limited

Printed and bound in Italy by
New Interlitho, Milan

# CONTENTS

*4* MAPPING THE PAST

*6* WHERE PEOPLE LIVED

*8* CLUES TO THE PAST

*10* SUMER – THE FIRST CITIES

*12* EGYPT – LIFE ON THE NILE

*14* EGYPT – PHARAOHS
AND PYRAMIDS

*16* INDUS VALLEY
CIVILIZATION

*18* EUROPE – THE MONUMENT
BUILDERS

*20* MINOANS AND MYCENAEANS

*22* CANAAN – LAND OF PLENTY

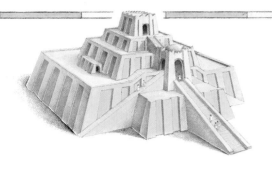

23 KINGDOMS OF THE HEBREWS

24 PHOENICIANS – RULERS OF THE SEA

26 BABYLON – GATE OF THE GODS

28 ASSYRIANS – KINGS OF CONQUEST

30 CELTS – IRON AGE HEROES

32 PERSIA – THE MAGNIFICENT EMPIRE

34 GREECE – THE POWER AND THE GLORY

36 GREECE – ALEXANDER AND AFTER

38 ROME – FROM VILLAGES TO EMPIRE

40 ROME – LIFE IN THE CITY

42 THE RICHES OF ARABIA

44 AFRICA – KINGDOMS OF GOLD

46 INDIA – THE MAURYAN AGE

48 CHINA – THE FIRST EMPEROR

50 NORTH AMERICAN PEOPLES

52 THE FIRST AUSTRALIANS

53 POLYNESIA AND NEW ZEALAND

54 CHINA – THE GOLDEN AGE

56 JAPAN – RISE OF THE SAMURAI

57 KINGDOM OF THE KHMERS

58 MAYA – CITIES OF STONE

59 AZTECS – WARRIORS OF THE SUN

60 INCAS – LORDS OF THE ANDES

62 TIMECHART

64 INDEX

# MAPPING THE PAST

THIS ATLAS TELLS THE STORY of how people lived in the ancient world. It also shows where the world's greatest civilizations were located and how they developed in very different environments. The book starts in the Middle East in the hot, crowded cities of Sumer in 3500 BC and finishes high in the Andes Mountains of South America with the Incas in AD 1500. Each of the peoples included in the book have left their mark on history, often for very different reasons. The Egyptians, for example, built huge pyramid tombs, the Chinese introduced remarkable inventions, the Romans organized vast armies, and the Greeks developed theater and the Olympic Games.

### CIVILIZATIONS AND CULTURES

This book covers many different peoples – most of them described as civilizations. The word "civilization" is used for a group of people who have reached an advanced stage of development. This usually means they have organized methods of farming and a large population that is settled in towns and cities. They have developed a system of writing, worked out a method of government, and built large monuments for their gods and their rulers. But the word civilization is sometimes extended to cover other peoples, too. These may be groups who did not write, such as the Celts, or peoples who, like the Australian Aboriginals, preferred not to live in cities, but who still created a rich and unique culture of their own.

*Many of the early civilizations worshiped gods and goddesses. The Egyptians built huge decorated temples for their gods, some of whom are shown here.*

*When people did not have to spend all their time growing food, they were able to develop new skills. This craftworker is decorating a wooden coffin.*

*Craftworkers often used goods from other lands, such as wood, silver, and ivory.*

*Writing was one of the features of a civilization. The Egyptians used hieroglyphs to keep private and government records.*

*The first great civilizations grew in fertile river valleys. Water from the Nile River was guided into fields. Enough crops were produced to feed the growing population.*

This wall painting is from an Egyptian tomb. It shows some of the ways in which organized farming created the wealth necessary for a civilization to develop. The tomb was built in about 1290 BC for Sennedjem, one of the workers who decorated the tombs of the pharaohs.

*Mud from the river banks was shaped into bricks to build homes in the world's first cities.*

*Domesticated animals made life easier for ancient peoples. Cattle pulled the plows used to prepare the ground for sowing.*

*Egyptian agriculture was so successful that farmers were able to grow a wide range of food, including date palms.*

*As society developed some people became very wealthy. They could afford fine linen clothes made from these flax plants.*

*The invention of tools helped farmers to be more efficient. Workers used wooden-handled sickles with flint blades to cut the grain.*

### DATING SYSTEMS

Throughout the book you will find references to the Stone Age, the Bronze Age, and the Iron Age. These divisions of history are based on the tools and weapons most used by a particular civilization. They cannot be used to identify a specific date worldwide because they happened at different times. The Bronze Age in the Middle East, for example, began hundreds of years earlier than in China. Elsewhere in the text, dates after the names of rulers such as King Darius (522-486 BC) give the time of their reign. Dates are also divided into BC (meaning before Christ) or AD (*anno domini*, meaning after the birth of Christ). An approximate date is shown as c.1200 BC (c. stands for *circa*, or about).

This model shows a Greek warrior from the Iron Age.

The Great Wall of China was built as a border to protect the Chinese from invaders in the north. Features such as mountain ranges or rivers also created natural barriers between territories.

### THE CHANGING WORLD

Many of the landscapes shown in this book do not look the same today. Over thousands of years, rivers alter their courses, new islands are born when a volcano erupts under the sea, and coastlines change. The ancient city of Ephesus, once on the Mediterranean coast, became silted up and now lies further inland. People can change the landscape, too. At one time Europe was covered in thick forests, long since chopped down for fuel and building materials. Before being overused, the northern edge of the Sahara Desert was fertile enough to provide crops for Rome. During the period covered by this book, borders between territories have also changed many times.

## HOW TO USE THE ATLAS

Each of the maps in this book looks at a different civilization, such as the Roman Empire shown below. Each map features the towns, cities, and trade routes that were important at the time. Small scenes of daily life are located as closely as possible to where they happened. The maps also show the physical features – deserts, mountains, lakes, forests, and marshes – that affected how people lived.

**Surrounding areas**
Areas that are shown in the pale yellow color are not part of the civilization featured on those pages. These areas are included to show the lands, and possible enemies, that lay beyond the territory of the people.

**Special features**
Many of the pages in the atlas have special illustrated scenes which explain part of the story on that page. This view shows the layout of a Roman army camp. Other views might show the interior of a house, a street scene, or a reconstruction of the layout of a city.

**Where in the world**
On each map there is a globe. The red shaded area on this globe shows the location in the world of the civilization featured on that map.

### KEY TO MAP

**Alexandria**

The location of towns and cities are marked with a red dot, together with the place name.

**Byzantium (Istanbul)**

If a town has a different modern name it may be shown in parentheses underneath.

**ITALICA**

Symbols, such as this amphitheater, are used to show the location of ancient sites or buildings.

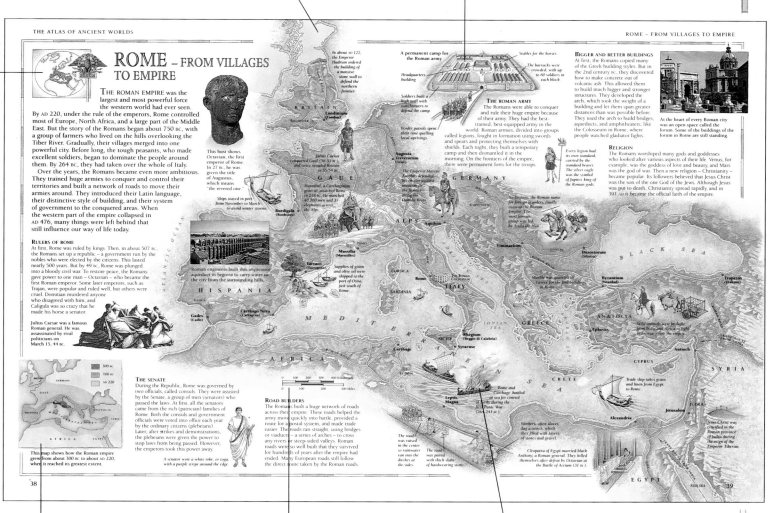

**Spread of an empire**
On some pages there are small inset maps. These show how an empire expanded beyond the area shown on the main map. Areas are shown in different colors with dates to explain when that part of the empire was conquered.

**Scale guide**
You can use this scale to determine the size of the area shown on the map. You can also calculate the length of an ancient road or the distance from one city to another. Not all the maps are drawn to the same scale.

**Detailed scenes**
On every map, there are scenes to show how people passed their time – fighting, working, playing, or worshiping their gods. Each scene, such as this sea battle, is located as closely as possible to the place where it would have happened.

### AN ANCIENT VIEW OF THE WORLD

The maps in this book are based on modern mapping techniques. Before the world was mapped out as it is today, people only understood the extent of the world as they knew it. Cartographers (mapmakers) based maps on their own experience, and unknown territory was often shown as being full of terrifying creatures. They always put the direction they thought was most important at the top. Many people's ideas of the world were based on their beliefs about how their gods created the world. The ancient East Indians, for example, believed the world was supported on the back of a turtle.

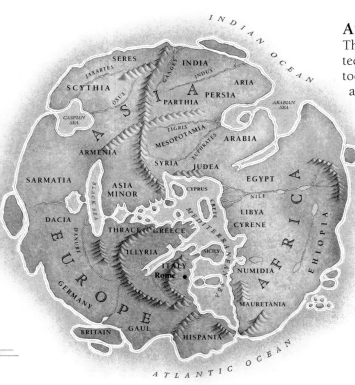

This artwork is based on a Roman map of the world from the 1st century BC. It shows how mapmakers thought the Roman Empire took up most of the world. They placed Rome near the center with Asia at the top, Africa to the right, and Europe to the left.

The Arab mapmaker al-Idrisi made this map of the world in AD 1154. Unlike the Romans, the Arabs liked to put south at the top.

# WHERE PEOPLE LIVED

MANY THOUSANDS OF YEARS AGO, people wandered the world in search of food, finding shelter in caves or in tents made of animal skins. They hunted animals and gathered fruits, nuts, and whatever vegetables they could find. Around 10,000 BC, the first farming began within an arc of land known as the Fertile Crescent in the Middle East. Gradually, farming spread throughout Europe. It also developed independently in other areas of the world, including the Americas, Africa, and the Far East. Farming enabled people to control their food supply. For the first time, they could stay in one place all year round. Villages and towns began to develop.

By about 3500 BC, the time when this book starts, people had begun to settle. Soon the first great civilization – Sumer – sprang up between the rivers Tigris and Euphrates in modern-day Iraq. Over the next 5,000 years, the period of time covered by this book, the civilizations shown on these maps developed around the world.

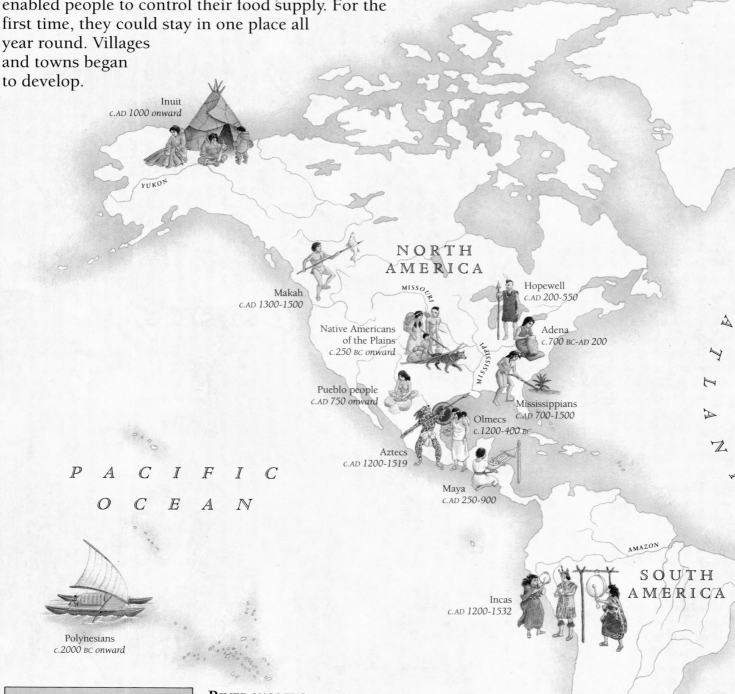

Inuit
c.AD 1000 onward

YUKON

Makah
c.AD 1300-1500

NORTH
AMERICA

MISSOURI

Hopewell
c.AD 200-550

Native Americans
of the Plains
c.250 BC onward

Adena
c.700 BC-AD 200

MISSISSIPPI

Pueblo people
c.AD 750 onward

Mississippians
c.AD 700-1500

Olmecs
c.1200-400 BC

Aztecs
c.AD 1200-1519

Maya
c.AD 250-900

Celts
c.750 BC-AD 100

Monument Builders
c.2500-1000 BC

Ghana
c.AD 700-1200

NIGER

ATLANTIC OCEAN

PACIFIC
OCEAN

Polynesians
c.2000 BC onward

AMAZON

SOUTH
AMERICA

Incas
c.AD 1200-1532

This scene from Iraq shows the fertile land and mud-brick houses along the River Tigris.

### RIVER VALLEYS

It is no coincidence that the first great civilizations – Sumer, Egypt, China, and the Indus Valley – all grew along large rivers. There were enormous advantages. Besides offering a constant supply of fresh water for crops, the rivers provided a way to transport heavy materials for building, and a route for boats to bring goods from abroad. People prospered and populations grew. Farmers produced so much food that people were free to develop specialized skills – they became potters, weavers, metal workers, and builders.

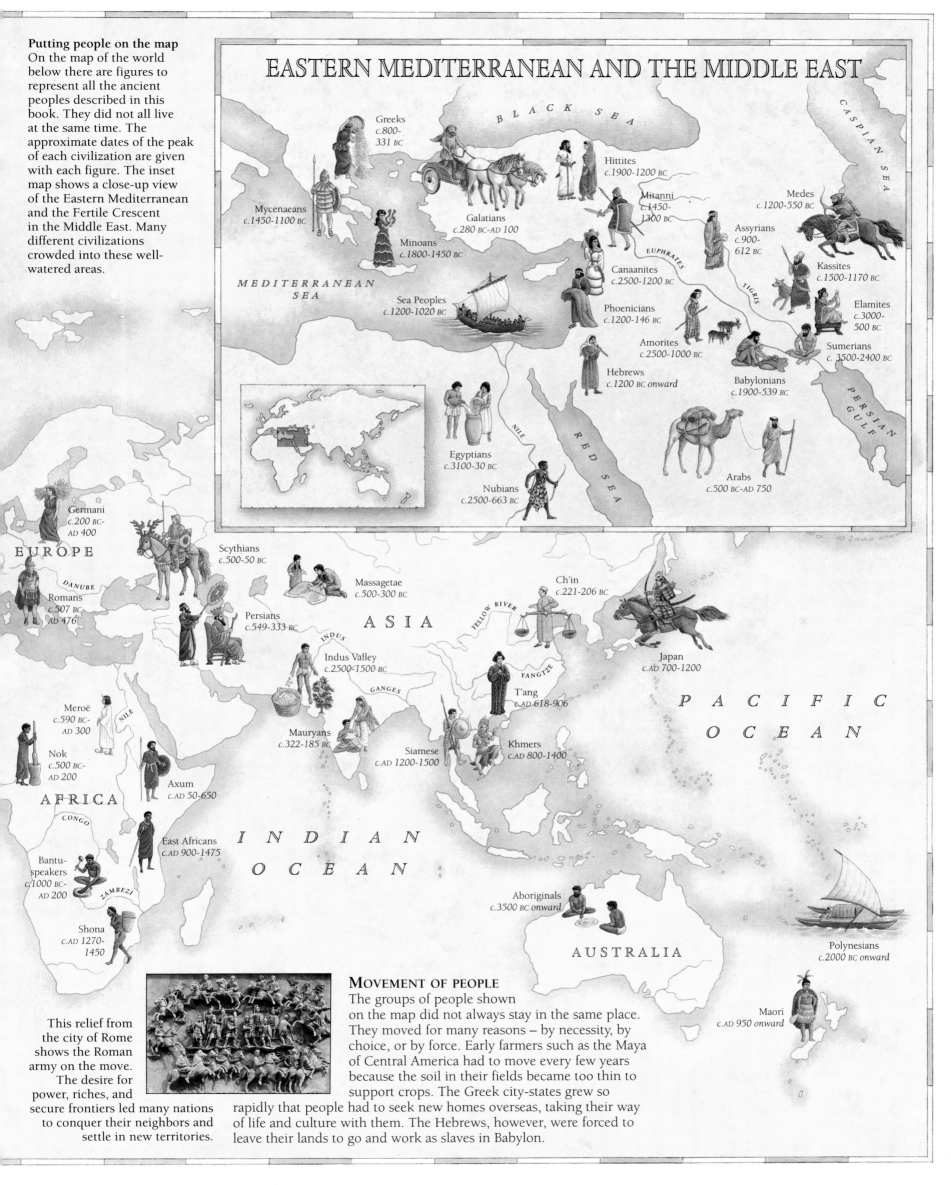

**Putting people on the map**
On the map of the world below there are figures to represent all the ancient peoples described in this book. They did not all live at the same time. The approximate dates of the peak of each civilization are given with each figure. The inset map shows a close-up view of the Eastern Mediterranean and the Fertile Crescent in the Middle East. Many different civilizations crowded into these well-watered areas.

# EASTERN MEDITERRANEAN AND THE MIDDLE EAST

BLACK SEA

Greeks
c.800-
331 BC

Hittites
c.1900-1200 BC

Mitanni
c.1450-
1300 BC

CASPIAN SEA

Medes
c.1200-550 BC

Galatians
c.280 BC-AD 100

Mycenaeans
c.1450-1100 BC

Minoans
c.1800-1450 BC

EUPHRATES

Assyrians
c.900-
612 BC

Kassites
c.1500-1170 BC

MEDITERRANEAN
SEA

Canaanites
c.2500-1200 BC

TIGRIS

Elamites
c.3000-
500 BC

Sea Peoples
c.1200-1020 BC

Phoenicians
c.1200-146 BC

Amorites
c.2500-1000 BC

Sumerians
c. 3500-2400 BC

Hebrews
c.1200 BC onward

Babylonians
c.1900-539 BC

PERSIAN
GULF

NILE

Arabs
c.500 BC-AD 750

Egyptians
c.3100-30 BC

RED SEA

Nubians
c.2500-663 BC

Germani
c.200 BC-
AD 400

EUROPE

Scythians
c.500-50 BC

DANUBE

Massagetae
c.500-300 BC

Ch'in
c.221-206 BC

Romans
c.507 BC-
AD 476

Persians
c.549-333 BC

ASIA

YELLOW RIVER

Japan
c.AD 700-1200

INDUS

Indus Valley
c.2500-1500 BC

PACIFIC
OCEAN

Meroë
c.590 BC-
AD 300

NILE

GANGES

YANGTZE

T'ang
c.AD 618-906

Nok
c.500 BC-
AD 200

Mauryans
c.322-185 BC

AFRICA

Axum
c.AD 50-650

Siamese
c.AD 1200-1500

Khmers
c.AD 800-1400

CONGO

East Africans
c.AD 900-1475

INDIAN
OCEAN

Bantu-
speakers
c.1000 BC-
AD 200

ZAMBEZI

Shona
c.AD 1270-
1450

Aboriginals
c.3500 BC onward

AUSTRALIA

Polynesians
c.2000 BC onward

Maori
c.AD 950 onward

This relief from the city of Rome shows the Roman army on the move. The desire for power, riches, and secure frontiers led many nations to conquer their neighbors and settle in new territories.

## MOVEMENT OF PEOPLE
The groups of people shown on the map did not always stay in the same place. They moved for many reasons – by necessity, by choice, or by force. Early farmers such as the Maya of Central America had to move every few years because the soil in their fields became too thin to support crops. The Greek city-states grew so rapidly that people had to seek new homes overseas, taking their way of life and culture with them. The Hebrews, however, were forced to leave their lands to go and work as slaves in Babylon.

# CLUES TO THE PAST

THIS BOOK IS FULL OF AMAZING DETAILS about people who lived thousands of years ago. But how do historians piece the information together – how do they find out what buildings were like, what clothes people wore, where they traded, and what they grew for food?

The experts who study the lives of ancient people from the remains of what they built or made are called archaeologists. Material remains and written records form the basis for most of our knowledge about the past.

Sometimes these experts are lucky enough to find the remains of ancient buildings still standing – like the Colosseum in Rome. More often, they have to dig to find walls and objects buried underground. Clues on the surface, such as coins or pieces of pottery, may suggest that an archaeological site is buried below. Other sites can be discovered by accident. For example, life-size warriors of a terra-cotta army were found in China by workers who were digging a well.

## MATERIAL EVIDENCE
Archaeologists learn about the past from objects people left behind. These may be the contents of graves, such as the furniture, gold jewelry, and musical instruments found in the royal tombs of Ur. Stone carvings from the palaces of Assyria and Persia reveal details of life at the royal courts. Coins are often inscribed with the names and dates of rulers, so they can be used to date the sites where they are found. Experts can also learn what people ate by analyzing the contents of their garbage dumps.

This map shows places where Greek pottery has been found. Finds like this give archaeologists valuable information about ancient trading networks. Experts can also find out where pottery was made by checking the color of the clay against a special soil color chart.

Paintings on pottery can tell us about daily life and what people wore in the ancient world. This Greek vase shows the olive harvest. Olives were pressed and the oil was used for cooking.

## WRITTEN RECORDS
Sometimes archaeologists have written records to help them. If an ancient people had a system of writing – and used materials that have survived, such as stone or clay tablets – archaeologists can learn about people's thoughts and beliefs, as well as practical information such as the names of rulers, dates of battles, and lists of items paid as taxes. The problem is that most ancient languages, except Latin, Greek, and Chinese, are no longer used, so their meaning has been lost. Experts have to learn how to read them – like the picture signs, or glyphs, of the ancient Maya, which have only recently been decoded.

*Hieroglyphics*

*Demotic writing*

Discovered by a French scholar in Napoleon's army, the Rosetta Stone held the key to deciphering Egyptian hieroglyphics. The same inscription was written three times – in hieroglyphics and demotic (two ancient Egyptian scripts), and in Greek. In all three, the name of Ptolemy (see right) appears. Applying the Greek letters in Ptolemy's name to the other signs was the first step in deciphering the hieroglyphics.

*Ancient Greek*

Hieroglyphics

Demotic writing

Ancient Greek

### Reconstructing a wooden house

A dark patch where wood has rotted may be the site of an old wooden posthole.

The depth of the hole may indicate the size of the post. An architect can calculate the height of the walls.

Details can then be filled in from other remains, such as the branches and mud, called wattle and daub, used to build walls.

*Daub*
*Wattle*

## BUILT TO LAST
In the past, people built their houses and monuments out of whatever materials were available. This could mean reeds and mud from the river, as in Sumer, or timber from the forests in Northern Europe. Most people did not worry whether their homes would outlast them, but when they built for the gods they wanted structures that would last forever. Thus, temples like those in Egypt or Mexico were built of stone. In Sumer, builders used bricks baked hard in the sun. Although great stone buildings have often survived, the homes of ordinary people have not. But some evidence may survive, and experts can reconstruct how these homes might have looked.

This Maya stone temple was discovered at Palenque, Mexico, in 1952. It has survived being overgrown by the rain forest.

Modern science can identify a mummy's blood type, even from dried-up blood vessels.

Experts have found fragments of false hair that were used to pad out thinning hair.

Remains from some Egyptian mummies show that people suffered from abscesses in their teeth.

Blood vessels near the heart and in the head reveal evidence of heart attacks and strokes.

Broken arms and legs that have been set show the skill (or otherwise) of the doctors.

Worms and parasites that once made a person's life miserable have been found preserved in mummies.

Legs and arms also show that people in the past suffered from arthritis and rheumatism, as they do today.

Some royal mummies have no name on them. It is hoped that DNA will help identify a mummy by revealing who its closest relatives were.

Sores and rashes can be found on the skin. They might be the result of a poor diet.

The Egyptians deliberately preserved dead bodies, which we call mummies. The body on the left shows what an Egyptian mummy looks like when unwrapped. This woman was probably buried some time around 600 BC. Even though some internal organs were removed, experts can still learn many things about the health and life-style of the ancient Egyptians.

## PRESERVED BY NATURE

There are certain natural elements which preserve things for longer than usual. The dry heat in Egypt has helped to preserve bodies and objects placed in tombs. At the other extreme, the frozen body of a man who died almost 5,000 years ago was found in the Alps, still carrying a copper ax and wearing his boots. Under the right conditions salt water can also preserve objects, such as the Mycenaean ship and its contents which sank off the Greek coast at Ulu Burun. In a more dramatic way, the eruption of Mount Vesuvius in AD 79 threw out hot ash that preserved many objects that would not normally have survived.

## FACE MAPPING

Thanks to mummification, we can look into the faces of people who lived in ancient Egypt. Now specialists can reconstruct a human face from the remains of a skull. This process is known as "face mapping." First a plaster cast is made of the skull. Then, based on the shape of the skull, the face muscles are built up with modeling clay. The clay is kept damp so it can be pinched into shape. A layer of material to represent flesh is then added and features are marked in. The artworks on the right show how experts recently reconstructed a 2,300-year-old skull, now thought to be Princess Ada, a friend of Alexander the Great.

The expert starts with a skull. The jaw and remaining teeth will help determine the shape of the mouth.

A plaster cast is made and pegs are used as a guide for the levels of muscle on the face. The building-up process begins.

Flesh is laid over the muscle. Ears, eyes, and nose are added to give a lifelike appearance.

Hair is added and the flesh is painted to give the face natural tones.

## MODERN DATING TECHNIQUES

Once items are discovered they need to be dated. If an ancient people could write, we can usually date events in their history from their inscriptions. With other civilizations, experts can give approximate dates to different layers on an archaeological site by comparing finds with those from a culture that they can date. More precise dating can be achieved using modern techniques. Radiocarbon dating measures the radioactivity given off by carbon 14 atoms – the older the object, the less radioactivity. This method is used to date the remains of plants and animals. Thermoluminescence measures the light released from pottery objects. Some other techniques used for dating are shown here.

Aerial photography, shown at left, can reveal signs of ancient sites beneath the ground. Crops grow taller and greener where the soil is deeper. These crop marks in England indicate Roman fields and drainage ditches still there beneath the soil.

Archaeologists do not want to unwrap every mummy they find. In the past, X-rays have been helpful, but now they can use a computed tomography (CT) scan. This photo shows a mummy case entering a scanner, which may tell its sex, age, and cause of death.

With a powerful microscope, experts can identify ancient pollen grains (shown right) found in the soil of excavations. They can tell what plants and trees were growing, what the ancient landscape probably looked like, and what people ate.

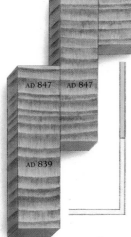

Dendrochronology is dating by counting tree rings. As trees grow, they form rings in the trunk. In good years the rings are wide, in bad years, narrow. When experts find wood from various periods where some rings match, they count back from the present and date the piece accurately.

AD 862
AD 856   AD 856
AD 847   AD 847
AD 839

# SUMER – THE FIRST CITIES

MORE THAN 5,000 YEARS AGO, the world's first cities were already crowded, bustling places. Situated around the Tigris and Euphrates rivers in what is now Iraq, cities such as Ur, Nippur, and Eridu had thousands of inhabitants. Within the heart of each city, a tall temple tower, built to provide a home for the god, rose above the sprawl of mud brick houses and workshops.

The area between the Tigris and Euphrates – later called Mesopotamia, which means "land between two rivers" – was extremely fertile. This rich land attracted the group of people we call Sumerians to settle there in about 5000 BC. Although the weather was hot and dry, the rivers supplied the Sumerians with all the water they needed to grow wheat, fruit, and vegetables. Their merchants traveled abroad, trading surplus food and beautiful items made by local artists. Gradually the population grew, and by about 3500 BC, the original farming villages had expanded into a number of city states, each with its own ruler.

Sumerians invented the wheel, which was used for shaping pottery. Then a wooden wheel was developed to move the first wheeled carts and chariots.

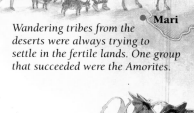

Wandering tribes from the deserts were always trying to settle in the fertile lands. One group that succeeded were the Amorites.

## THE BIG MAN

The affairs of a city were run by a Council of Elders. When war broke out, they appointed a *lugal*, meaning a "Big Man," to lead the army. As wars between the cities became more common, a *lugal* held onto power for longer periods of time, sometimes for life. He also started to control the daily life of his city. Finally, he began appointing his sons to take over for him. The "Big Men" had become kings.

This peaceful scene from the Standard of Ur, discovered in a royal grave, shows rulers celebrating at a banquet. Farmers bring cattle and sheep as gifts.

This copper relief from the temple at Ubaid shows a lion-headed eagle holding two stags by the tails. Copper, which was melted and poured into a mold, was also used to make weapons and tools.

## CITIES OF THE GODS

The Sumerians worshiped hundreds of gods, who they believed controlled different aspects of their lives. They made offerings each day to the gods, who they feared might otherwise punish them with unexpected floods, sickness, and wars. Each city also had a special god or goddess who was thought to own that city. For example, Enlil the storm god owned Nippur, while Enki the water god and god of wisdom lived in the city of Eridu.

## THE DEATH PITS OF UR

In the Sumerian city of Ur, archaeologists discovered the tombs of the early kings and queens. The remains showed what magnificent furniture, gold jewelry, musical instruments, and personal possessions the rulers owned. But that was not all. The tombs also contained the bodies of servants who had apparently agreed to commit suicide and be buried with their dead master or mistress, so they could serve them in the next world.

This magnificent gold headdress was found on the body of a court lady in one of the royal graves of Ur.

## STAIRWAY TO HEAVEN

At the heart of each city, there was a temple in which the god lived. The city of Ur, shown on the right, was home to the moon god Nanna. Very early temples were rectangular buildings erected on low platforms. Both temple and platform were made of sun-dried mud bricks. When a new temple was needed, it was built on top of the old one. This happened over and over again, until temple platforms, called ziggurats, became huge, stepped structures with the temple on top.

The ziggurat, or temple tower, at Ur was built by King Ur-Nammu, around 2100 BC.

Houses were built around open courtyards. There were no windows on the outside walls.

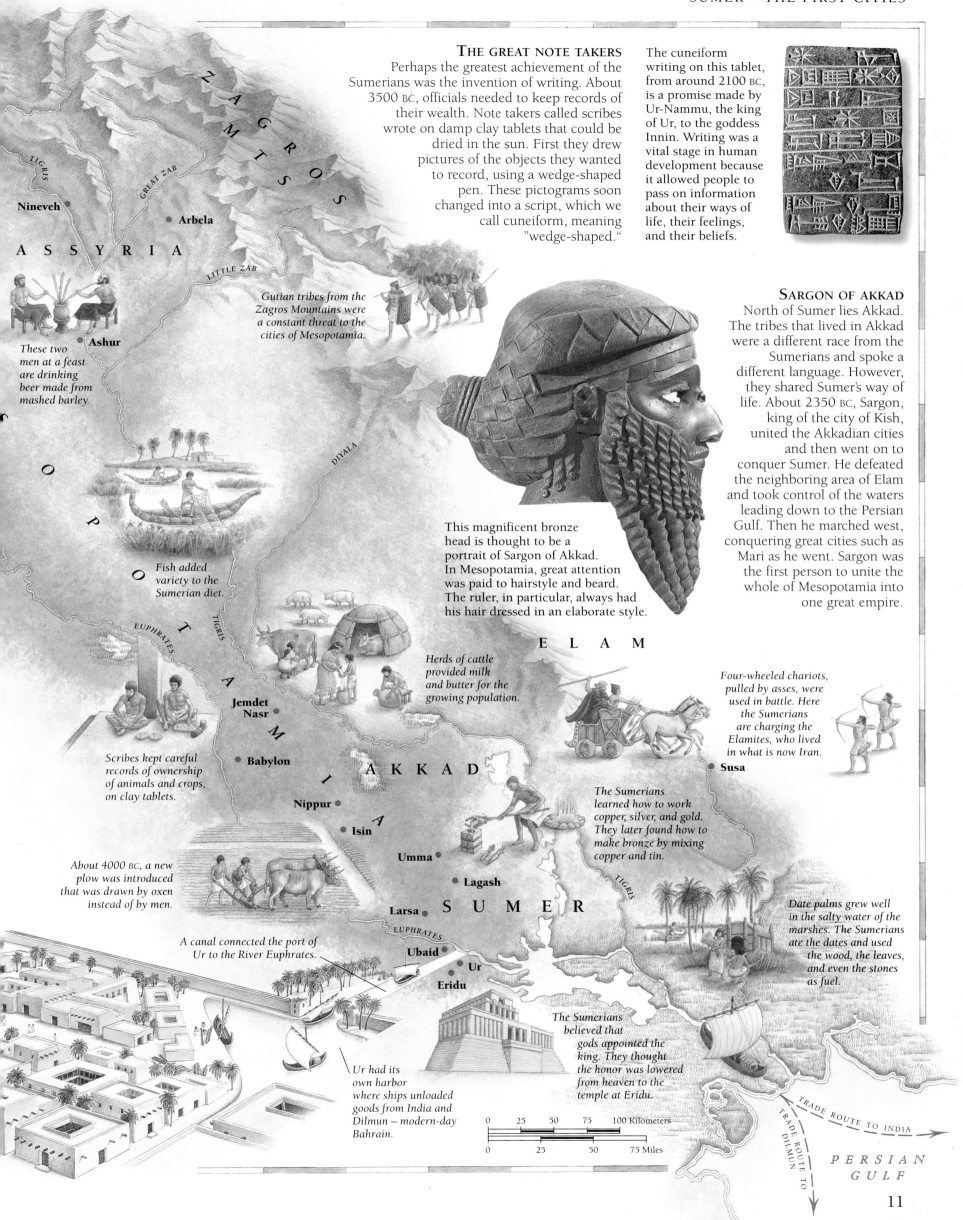

### THE GREAT NOTE TAKERS

Perhaps the greatest achievement of the Sumerians was the invention of writing. About 3500 BC, officials needed to keep records of their wealth. Note takers called scribes wrote on damp clay tablets that could be dried in the sun. First they drew pictures of the objects they wanted to record, using a wedge-shaped pen. These pictograms soon changed into a script, which we call cuneiform, meaning "wedge-shaped."

The cuneiform writing on this tablet, from around 2100 BC, is a promise made by Ur-Nammu, the king of Ur, to the goddess Innin. Writing was a vital stage in human development because it allowed people to pass on information about their ways of life, their feelings, and their beliefs.

*These two men at a feast are drinking beer made from mashed barley.*

*Gutian tribes from the Zagros Mountains were a constant threat to the cities of Mesopotamia.*

### SARGON OF AKKAD

North of Sumer lies Akkad. The tribes that lived in Akkad were a different race from the Sumerians and spoke a different language. However, they shared Sumer's way of life. About 2350 BC, Sargon, king of the city of Kish, united the Akkadian cities and then went on to conquer Sumer. He defeated the neighboring area of Elam and took control of the waters leading down to the Persian Gulf. Then he marched west, conquering great cities such as Mari as he went. Sargon was the first person to unite the whole of Mesopotamia into one great empire.

*Fish added variety to the Sumerian diet.*

*This magnificent bronze head is thought to be a portrait of Sargon of Akkad. In Mesopotamia, great attention was paid to hairstyle and beard. The ruler, in particular, always had his hair dressed in an elaborate style.*

*Herds of cattle provided milk and butter for the growing population.*

*Four-wheeled chariots, pulled by asses, were used in battle. Here the Sumerians are charging the Elamites, who lived in what is now Iran.*

*Scribes kept careful records of ownership of animals and crops, on clay tablets.*

*The Sumerians learned how to work copper, silver, and gold. They later found how to make bronze by mixing copper and tin.*

*About 4000 BC, a new plow was introduced that was drawn by oxen instead of by men.*

*Date palms grew well in the salty water of the marshes. The Sumerians ate the dates and used the wood, the leaves, and even the stones as fuel.*

*A canal connected the port of Ur to the River Euphrates.*

*The Sumerians believed that gods appointed the king. They thought the honor was lowered from heaven to the temple at Eridu.*

*Ur had its own harbor where ships unloaded goods from India and Dilmun – modern-day Bahrain.*

| 0 | 25 | 50 | 75 | 100 Kilometers |
| 0 | | 25 | 50 | 75 Miles |

*PERSIAN GULF*

TRADE ROUTE TO INDIA

TRADE ROUTE TO DILMUN

# EGYPT – LIFE ON THE NILE

WITHOUT THE LIFE-GIVING waters of the Nile River, Egypt would be a desert, and there would have been no Egyptian civilization. Many thousands of years ago, groups of hunters moved into the Nile valley. They found large numbers of animals, birds, and fish, as well as a reliable supply of water in the Nile River. They began to settle in the valley and, in about 5000 BC, adopted farming as their way of life. As these farmers prospered, communities joined together to form two kingdoms – Upper (Southern) Egypt and Lower (Northern) Egypt.

Then, in about 3100 BC, the king of Upper Egypt conquered the north and united the two kingdoms. Once the kingdoms were joined, Egyptian culture blossomed. Along with the Sumerians, the Egyptians were one of the first peoples to invent a system of writing. Their sculptors and painters produced many works of art; and their architects built enormous temples and pyramids.

## THE NILE IN FLOOD

Every year summer rains in the mountains at the source of the Nile caused the river to overflow farther down in the flat valley. The farmers learned how to dig canals and basins to store the floodwater. Later in the year they guided this water onto the fields through ditches. If it was a "good Nile" the floodwaters covered the land with rich, black mud that fertilized the fields.

## FOREIGN TRADE

Thanks to the annual flood, the Egyptians could grow more food than they needed. They sold the surplus abroad. They traded with Canaan in the east, with Nubia and Punt to the south, and with Libya to the west. Later they traded goods with Crete and Greece and also with the Babylonian Empire. The Egyptians exported agricultural produce, linen, papyrus (a form of paper), and manufactured goods. They imported timber, incense, slaves, silver, horses, copper, tin, and wine.

*Horses, slaves, and pottery were imported from Palestine.*

An ancient Egyptian town had a marketplace where people went to buy food, pots, pans, and leather goods. Markets such as this one in Cairo have changed very little since ancient times.

## BOATS ON THE RIVER

The Nile River was Egypt's main highway. It provided an easy and efficient means of transporting people and goods. Small boats were made of bundles of reeds lashed together. Bigger boats were made of wood held together with wooden pegs and ropes. The boats could be taken apart and carried across the Eastern Desert to the Red Sea, or around the great rocks that formed the Nile's cataracts (waterfalls). They were then rebuilt and put back into the water.

Modern-day Egyptians still use the Nile as a trade route, carrying goods on boats such as this felucca.

### Map labels

MEDITERRANEAN SEA

TRADE ROUTE TO CANAAN

TRADE ROUTE TO LIBYA

OVERLAND ROUTE TO COPPER AND TURQUOISE MINES

SINAI

RED SEA

TRADE ROUTE TO PUNT

WESTERN DESERT

EASTERN DESERT

NILE DELTA

NILE

E G Y P T

Sais
Tanis
Avaris
Giza
Memphis
Saqqara
FAIYUM OASIS
Heracleopolis
Beni Hasan
El-Amarna
Abydos
Dendera
Coptos
Thebes
Armant
Hieraconpolis

*Cattle were driven up to high ground to avoid the Nile floods.*

*Papyrus*

*Egyptian fields were divided into small plots by the irrigation ditches.*

*Plowing fields*

*Harvesting grain*

*Fishing on the Nile*

*Grain was stored in huge terra-cotta (clay) jars.*

*Date palms*

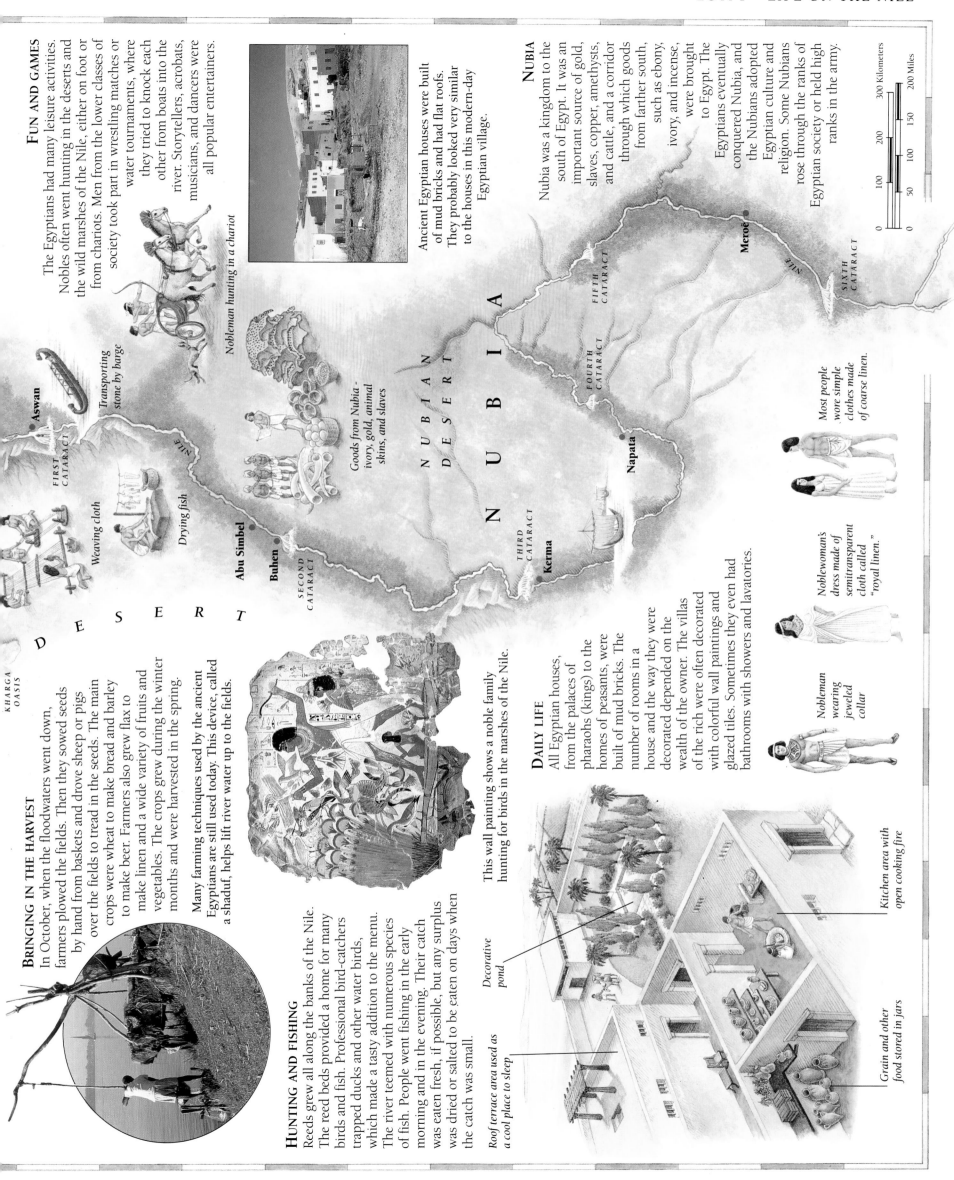

## FUN AND GAMES

The Egyptians had many leisure activities. Nobles often went hunting in the deserts and the wild marshes of the Nile, either on foot or from chariots. Men from the lower classes of society took part in wrestling matches or water tournaments, where they tried to knock each other from boats into the river. Storytellers, acrobats, musicians, and dancers were all popular entertainers.

*Nobleman hunting in a chariot*

*Transporting stone by barge*

*Weaving cloth*

*Drying fish*

Ancient Egyptian houses were built of mud bricks and had flat roofs. They probably looked very similar to the houses in this modern-day Egyptian village.

## NUBIA

Nubia was a kingdom to the south of Egypt. It was an important source of gold, slaves, copper, amethysts, and cattle, and a corridor through which goods from farther south, such as ebony, ivory, and incense, were brought to Egypt. The Egyptians eventually conquered Nubia, and the Nubians adopted Egyptian culture and religion. Some Nubians rose through the ranks of Egyptian society or held high ranks in the army.

*Goods from Nubia - ivory, gold, animal skins, and slaves*

**Aswan**

FIRST CATARACT

**Abu Simbel**

**Buhen**

SECOND CATARACT

KHARGA OASIS

D E S E R T

N U B I A N   D E S E R T

N U B I A

**Kerma**

THIRD CATARACT

**Napata**

FOURTH CATARACT

FIFTH CATARACT

**Meroë**

SIXTH CATARACT

NILE

0   100   200   300 Kilometers

0   50   100   150   200 Miles

*Most people wore simple clothes made of coarse linen.*

*Noblewoman's dress made of semitransparent cloth called "royal linen."*

*Nobleman wearing jeweled collar*

## BRINGING IN THE HARVEST

In October, when the floodwaters went down, farmers plowed the fields. Then they sowed seeds by hand from baskets and drove sheep or pigs over the fields to tread in the seeds. The main crops were wheat to make bread and barley to make beer. Farmers also grew flax to make linen and a wide variety of fruits and vegetables. The crops grew during the winter months and were harvested in the spring.

Many farming techniques used by the ancient Egyptians are still used today. This device, called a shaduf, helps lift river water up to the fields.

## HUNTING AND FISHING

Reeds grew all along the banks of the Nile. The reed beds provided a home for many birds and fish. Professional bird-catchers trapped ducks and other water birds, which made a tasty addition to the menu. The river teemed with numerous species of fish. People went fishing in the early morning and in the evening. Their catch was eaten fresh, if possible, but any surplus was dried or salted to be eaten on days when the catch was small.

This wall painting shows a noble family hunting for birds in the marshes of the Nile.

## DAILY LIFE

All Egyptian houses, from the palaces of pharaohs (kings) to the homes of peasants, were built of mud bricks. The number of rooms in a house and the way they were decorated depended on the wealth of the owner. The villas of the rich were often decorated with colorful wall paintings and glazed tiles. Sometimes they even had bathrooms with showers and lavatories.

*Decorative pond*

*Roof terrace area used as a cool place to sleep*

*Kitchen area with open cooking fire*

*Grain and other food stored in jars*

# EGYPT – PHARAOHS AND PYRAMIDS

THE MOST IMPORTANT PERSON in Egypt was the pharaoh, or king. At one time, he was thought to be so powerful that it was dangerous to touch him even by accident. The Egyptians believed that when their king was seated on the throne holding the symbols of power, the spirit of the hawk-headed god Horus entered him, and he became god on earth. He was responsible for the well-being of Egypt and for making sure the country was run as the gods intended. As the person on earth who housed the god's spirit, the king was always treated with great respect.

The Egyptians believed in life after death. When a king died, his body was placed in a special tomb, called a pyramid, with clothes, furniture, jewelry, and personal belongings for the dead person to use in the next world. The first pyramids had steps on the outside, so the king could climb up them to join the gods. However, religious beliefs changed, and pyramids became straight-sided. Later kings were buried in magnificently decorated tombs cut into the rock of the cliffs in the Valley of Kings, to hide them from grave robbers.

The warrior pharaohs of the New Kingdom conquered the greatest empire of their day. This map shows the extent of the area under Egyptian rule around 1400 BC.

### THE RULE OF THE PHARAOHS
Pharaohs ruled Egypt for about 3,000 years. Historians divide this long period of history into the Old, Middle, and New Kingdoms. As the king of Egypt was believed to be descended from the gods, it was difficult to know who was good enough to be his queen. He could have many wives, but his queen (known as Great Royal Wife) had to be royal so the blood of the gods was not diluted. For this reason, kings often married their sisters or a close female relative. Their eldest son would become the next pharaoh.

The ankh was the Egyptian symbol of life. It was carried as a popular amulet, or good luck charm.

One of the early pharaohs of the New Kingdom was the successful ruler Queen Hatshepsut. When her husband died, she pushed her stepson Tuthmosis III aside and made herself "king" of Egypt.

**KEY TO MAP**

Pyramid

Temple

Tomb

Obelisk

King Tutankhamun and Queen Ankhesenamun relax under the rays of the sun god.

Senusret III was one of the great warrior pharaohs of the Middle Kingdom. His army headed south, conquered the Nubians, and strengthened the frontier fortresses.

### AFFAIRS OF STATE
The king of Egypt had many important roles. As head of the government, he controlled the law, the army, and the cults of all the gods. At important festivals, he performed the temple rituals himself, so the people could see him as a god-king. With his queen, he welcomed foreign princes who brought gifts to the court. To help him govern, he had two chief ministers (for Upper and Lower Egypt) and an army of officials, scribes, and priests who took care of the day-to-day running of the country.

*Anubis, jackal-headed guardian of the dead*

*The sun god as Khepri the scarab beetle*

*Horus, hawk-headed sky god*

*Thoth, god of wisdom, with his ibis head*

*Osiris, god of the dead*

### HOMES OF THE GODS
The Egyptians had many gods and goddesses to take care of their problems and grant their wishes. Many of these gods were shown with a human body and the head of the bird or animal that represented its power. A statue of the god was placed in a sanctuary and was only removed for religious ceremonies. The Egyptians built huge, beautifully decorated temples as earthly homes for their gods. The greatest god in the New Kingdom was Amun, king of the gods, whose temple at Karnak still stands.

The royal blue war helmet

The bow and arrow were often used.

The ceremonial battle-ax had a fancy carved blade.

Chariots were made of wood and bronze.

A New Kingdom pharaoh rode into battle. Chariots were introduced into Egypt by invaders from the northeast called the Hyksos.

Two decorated horses pulled each chariot.

The short sword was part of a New Kingdom soldier's basic equipment.

## THE EGYPTIAN ARMY

In the Old and Middle Kingdoms, Egypt had only a small army of foot soldiers to protect its frontiers. If there was a national emergency, extra men could be called up for duty. In the New Kingdom, however, the horse and chariot were used for the first time, and the army was transformed into a large, permanent force ready to conquer an empire.

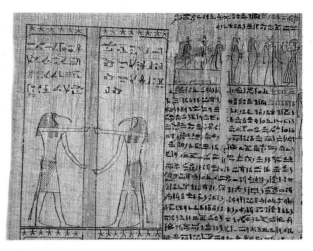

This ancient papyrus shows hieroglyphs on the left. The easier-to-write hieratic script is used on the right.

## THE DEVELOPMENT OF WRITING

About 3300 BC, the Egyptians invented a system of writing using picture signs, which we call hieroglyphs. There were more than 700 picture signs to learn. Hieroglyphic script took a long time to write, so a shorthand version, called hieratic, was introduced. Scripts were written on a kind of paper made from the stems of the papyrus reed, that grew along the Nile River.

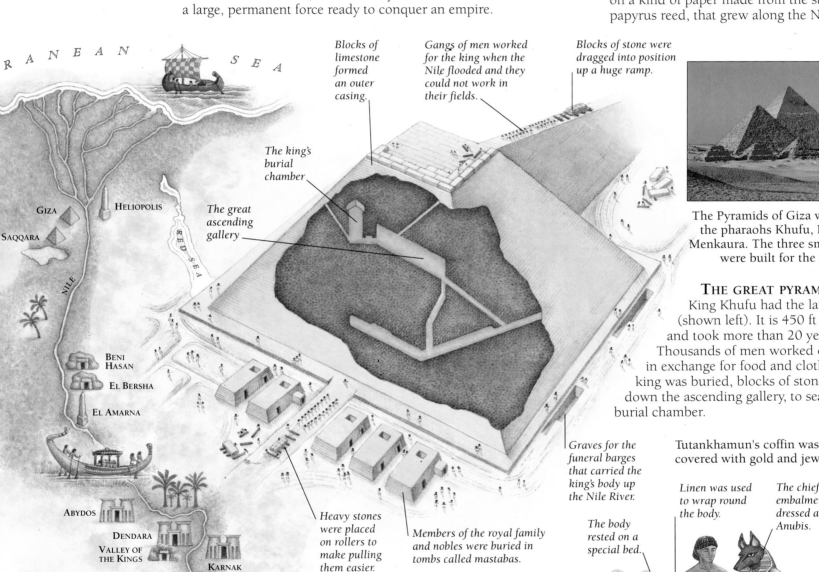

Blocks of limestone formed an outer casing.

Gangs of men worked for the king when the Nile flooded and they could not work in their fields.

Blocks of stone were dragged into position up a huge ramp.

The king's burial chamber

The great ascending gallery

The Pyramids of Giza were built for the pharaohs Khufu, Khafra, and Menkaura. The three small pyramids were built for the queens.

## THE GREAT PYRAMID

King Khufu had the largest pyramid (shown left). It is 450 ft (146 m) tall and took more than 20 years to build. Thousands of men worked on the tomb in exchange for food and clothes. Once the king was buried, blocks of stone were slid down the ascending gallery, to seal off his burial chamber.

Heavy stones were placed on rollers to make pulling them easier.

Members of the royal family and nobles were buried in tombs called mastabas.

Graves for the funeral barges that carried the king's body up the Nile River.

Tutankhamun's coffin was covered with gold and jewels.

Linen was used to wrap round the body.

The chief embalmer dressed as Anubis.

The body rested on a special bed.

## BURIAL CUSTOMS

The Egyptians believed that to enjoy life after death their bodies had to survive, so they invented the process we call mummification. First, the internal organs were removed and stored in special jars. The corpse was covered with a local salt (natron) that prevented decay. After the body had dried out, it was packed with linen and spices to fill out its original shape, then bandaged and placed in an elaborate coffin.

Internal organs were stored in canopic jars.

Jewels for the dead person to take to the next world

### Death on the Nile

This map shows the position along the Nile River of some of the surviving pyramids, rock-cut tombs, and temples of ancient Egypt. The obelisk, symbol of the sun god Re, was erected in front of all the main temples.

GIZA
HELIOPOLIS
SAQQARA
BENI HASAN
EL BERSHA
EL AMARNA
ABYDOS
DENDARA
VALLEY OF THE KINGS
KARNAK
EDFU
KOM OMBO (ASWAN)

# INDUS VALLEY CIVILIZATION

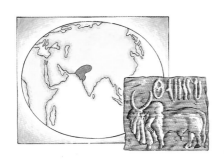

A rare statue from the city of Mohenjo-Daro shows the bearded face of a man, probably a priest. Experts think the priests may also have been the kings.

ALONG THE VALLEY OF THE INDUS RIVER in modern-day India and Pakistan, another great civilization had developed. For awhile, in about 2500 BC, it was one of the greatest civilizations in the world. Successful farmers grew crops in the fertile soil along the river and used mud from the river to make bricks for their buildings. Archaeologists have found the remains of two impressive cities – at Mohenjo-Daro and Harappa – which both had populations of up to 40,000 people. Inside the city walls, there was an artificial hill made of mud and bricks. Perched on top, local rulers lived in a large fortress that overlooked the city.

Despite these achievements, this society died out mysteriously in about 1500 BC, and many details of the Indus Valley people remain unknown. Experts have not been able to explain why this happened, nor have they managed to read the Indus Valley writing that could offer clues to the past.

Around 1500 BC, people called Indo-Aryans invaded the Indus Valley. This may have contributed to the collapse of the civilization.

The Indus people used spears to kill animals that would provide food for their families. They may also have hunted just for sport.

As in other great river valley civilizations, there was plenty of mud for bricks, as well as for pots. Strong bricks for large buildings were baked in a wood-fired kiln.

HINDU KUSH

I N D U S

Mohenjo-Daro

The Great Bath at Mohenjo-Daro was probably used to cleanse and purify rulers and priests before religious ceremonies.

Chanhu-Daro

Amri

Sutkagen-Dor

The farmers knew how to control the flooding of the Indus River and divert the water to their crops.

## CLEAN LIVING

The wealthy Indus Valley families lived in a comfortable house built around a courtyard. Stairs led to a flat roof, where there was extra space to work and relax. Although there was not much furniture, the homes had wells for water and bathrooms with pipes that carried waste into the main drains. Cleanliness was obviously very important, and bathing may have played a part in the religious rituals.

Fishing nets were probably made from cotton strong enough to catch sea fish.

The fortress, or citadel, where the important buildings were situated.

In the intense heat of summer, people often slept on the roof, where it was cooler.

**Inside a typical house in a Mohenjo-Daro street scene**

The roof was also used for drying crops for storage.

A R A B I A N   S E A

Beds were probably made from wooden frames fitted with woven leather strips, to provide support for the body.

Houses had separate toilets connected to the main drainage system.

A door opened onto the street, but windows always faced the courtyard for extra privacy.

Drains were laid under the streets. When they needed to be cleaned out, workers could get into the drains through inspection holes.

A wooden balcony overlooked the central courtyard.

Homes had their own wells. Cool water was drawn up when needed.

TRADE ROUTE TO SUMER

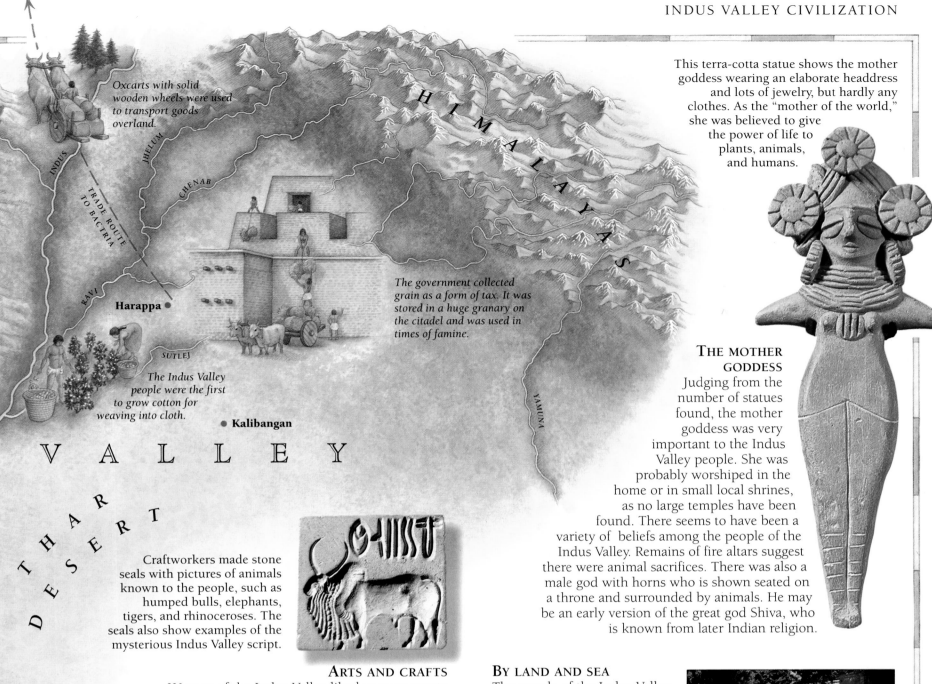

Oxcarts with solid wooden wheels were used to transport goods overland.

**TRADE ROUTE TO BACTRIA**

Harappa

The government collected grain as a form of tax. It was stored in a huge granary on the citadel and was used in times of famine.

The Indus Valley people were the first to grow cotton for weaving into cloth.

● Kalibangan

VALLEY

THAR DESERT

Craftworkers made stone seals with pictures of animals known to the people, such as humped bulls, elephants, tigers, and rhinoceroses. The seals also show examples of the mysterious Indus Valley script.

This terra-cotta statue shows the mother goddess wearing an elaborate headdress and lots of jewelry, but hardly any clothes. As the "mother of the world," she was believed to give the power of life to plants, animals, and humans.

## THE MOTHER GODDESS

Judging from the number of statues found, the mother goddess was very important to the Indus Valley people. She was probably worshiped in the home or in small local shrines, as no large temples have been found. There seems to have been a variety of beliefs among the people of the Indus Valley. Remains of fire altars suggest there were animal sacrifices. There was also a male god with horns who is shown seated on a throne and surrounded by animals. He may be an early version of the great god Shiva, who is known from later Indian religion.

## ARTS AND CRAFTS

Women of the Indus Valley liked to wear ornate necklaces, bangles, and earrings. This jewelry was made from gold, silver, shells, and stones such as carnelian, a red-colored quartz. The Indus pottery was also of good quality and was often red with black geometric or flower designs. Stone carvers produced some remarkable pieces made from soapstone, a soft whitish stone with a "soapy" feel to it. Soapstone was also used to make the seals that merchants used to mark their property.

## BY LAND AND SEA

The people of the Indus Valley were not entirely self-sufficient. They needed tin, which they mixed with copper to make bronze, and semiprecious stones for jewelry, which they imported overland from modern-day Afghanistan and Persia. The Indus traders also traveled overseas. On the coast at Lothal, there was a brick-built harbor, where merchant ships entered at high tide through a special channel. They unloaded goods into the warehouses by the docks. Traders paid with ivory, timber, cotton, gems, and spices.

Oxcarts are still used to transport heavy goods through the busy streets of Pakistan, the location of the Indus Valley civilization.

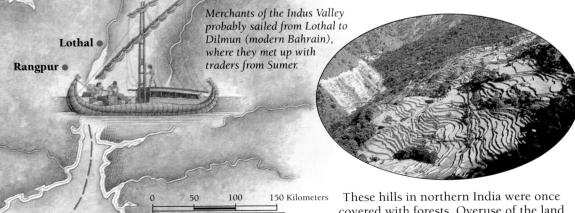

Lothal ■

Rangpur ●

Merchants of the Indus Valley probably sailed from Lothal to Dilmun (modern Bahrain), where they met up with traders from Sumer.

| 0 | 50 | 100 | 150 Kilometers |
| 0 | 25 | 50 | 75 | 100 Miles |

GULF OF CAMBAY

These hills in northern India were once covered with forests. Overuse of the land may also have ruined the Indus Valley.

## END OF AN ERA

No one is really sure of exactly what caused the decline of the Indus Valley civilization. Natural causes such as floods, droughts, and illness might have played a part. But the people themselves may have overused the land. As the population grew, they grazed more sheep and cows for food and clothes and chopped down more timber for cooking and building. Overuse of the land began to ruin the soil, so less food could be grown. The final blow may have been the arrival, around 1500 BC, of groups of people called Indo-Aryans who were seeking new homes.

# EUROPE – THE MONUMENT BUILDERS

MASSIVE BLOCKS OF STONE still stand in a large circle that forms the ancient monument known as Stonehenge in southern England. From about 2500-1000 BC, people across western Europe built great circles and long avenues of stones to honor their gods. They also dug great mounds of earth to mark the burial places of their honored dead. Although no records survive to explain these monuments, experts believe the stone circles may have been used for religious ceremonies or to follow the movement of the Sun and Moon.

But while great temples and glittering cities were being built elsewhere in the world, most Europeans preferred village life. Farming had spread to Europe, probably from Anatolia (modern Turkey), some time before 4000 BC. Thick forests were cut down to provide wood for building houses and to clear the ground for growing crops. The discovery of tin, which workers mixed with copper to make bronze, provided stronger tools and weapons. This was the beginning of Bronze Age Europe.

*Huts were round with thatched roofs.*

*A palisade (fence) of strong wooden stakes protected the village.*

*Villagers stored food in rooms on stilts to stop it from being eaten by rats.*

*Cattle were kept in pens inside the village so they would be safe from raiders.*

*Cutting wheat*

## VILLAGE LIFE

Most people in Europe settled in small villages or lived on isolated farms. They built houses from materials that could be found nearby, such as wood and thatch, or stone and turf. Some houses, near the lakes in Switzerland and northern Italy, were big enough for as many as 50 people. Farmers grew wheat and barley and kept cattle, pigs, sheep, and goats. Apples, plums, raspberries, and strawberries grew wild. We know a great deal about the food people ate from the remains found in their garbage heaps.

*The arch is called a trilithon. This means "three stones" in Greek.*

## SETTING UP STONEHENGE

Experts are still not sure of how Stonehenge was built. Construction started in about 2800 BC, when workers dug a henge – a circular ditch and bank of earth – that enclosed a ring of pits. Hundreds of years later, a double circle of "bluestones," thought to come from Wales, was added. By about 1600 BC, workers had replaced the bluestones with a ring of huge upright stones called sarsens and with groups of even larger stones in the center.

*Men built a cradle of logs under each stone to raise it into position as a crossbeam on two sarsens.*

*Gangs of workers lashed each stone to logs of wood or a sled. Then they pulled the stone along the ground, using the logs as rollers.*

*A sarsen (upright) being raised into position. Its base stood in a pit.*

*Much of Europe was covered with forests that had to be cleared when farmers needed more land.*

*Tin was much sought after and a valuable trading item. Much of it was mined in Spain.*

## DEAD AND BURIED

Like many ancient peoples, the monument builders believed in a life after death. Personal possessions, including pots and tools for the afterlife, have been found in their graves. Some men and women were buried under large earth mounds, known as barrows, with rich grave goods of gold and bronze. In about 1200 BC, a new culture, known as Urnfield, began to develop. When people died, they were cremated; their ashes were placed in urns that were left in cemeteries, known as urnfields.

*A local chief prepared for war with bronze weapons and armor.*

*Grain was ground between two stones to make flour.*

*A funeral procession winds its way to the spectacular burial mound at Los Millares.*

### KEY TO MAP

- Stone avenue
- Stone circle
- Burial site
- Tin mine

```
0    100   200   300   400 Kilometers
0   50   100  150  200  250 Miles
```

### Map labels

SHETLAND ISLANDS
Jarlshof
CALLANISH
HEBRIDES
SCOTLAND
IRELAND
BALLYNOE
Mold
BRENIG
WALES
Fengate
ENGLAND
Runnymede
STONEHENGE
ISLES OF SCILLY
ATLANTIC OCEAN
NO S
KERNONEN
Aulnay-aux Planches
CARNAC
ER LANNIC
SEINE
E
FRANCE
GARONNE
RHÔNE
Cortes de Navarra
EBRO
TAGUS
SPAIN
Los Millares
BALEARIC ISLANDS
ME E
AFRICA

*Fishermen often used hooks made of bones. They also used nets.*

SCANDINAVIA

*Rock carvings show us that Bronze Age Europeans had ships large enough to need several pairs of oars.*

● Hallunda

GULF OF BOTHNIA

H

BALTIC SEA

DENMARK

**Trundholm** ● KIVIK

*This horned helmet found in Denmark would not have been practical to wear in battle. It was probably only worn for ceremonies.*

● **Elp**

*Women collected amber from the Baltic seashore. It was used for making beads.*

ODER

RHINE

GERMANY

ELBE

HELMSDORF

*A smith pours liquid bronze into a mold to make an ax head.*

● **Blucina**

● **Barca**

USATOVE

J R O P E

**Wasserburg**

DANUBE

CAKA

*Some villages, such as the one at Wasserburg, were built out from the shores of the lake.*

SWITZERLAND

*Different cultures can be identified by their pottery. Urnfield pottery is found over a wide area of Europe.*

*The people of the Steppes were the first to tame horses. Europeans were quick to copy the idea.*

● **Monteoru**

BLACK SEA

DANUBE

**Gomolava** ●

*This figure of a Mother Goddess was found in southeast Europe. She is made of clay and has a full, bell-shaped skirt.*

**Varna** ●

*Water was poured onto copper ore so the copper could be removed.*

PO

A D R I A T I C   S E A

**Donja Slatina**

CORSICA

**Luni** ●

*Farmers used plows to prepare the land for growing wheat and barley.*

I T A L Y

GREECE

ANATOLIA

SARDINIA

**Scoglio del Tonno** ●

**Mycenae** ●

*A Mycenaean ship, with a cargo of amber from the Baltic Sea, heads for the eastern Mediterranean.*

T E R R A N E A N   S E A

SICILY

MALTA

CRETE

## TURNED TO BRONZE

The discovery of bronze, a mixture of copper and tin, had an enormous effect on the early Europeans. Until about 2000 BC, copper was used to make metal objects. But copper was too soft to make anything useful, such as tools and weapons; it was used mostly for ornamental items. By adding about 10 percent tin – which was mined in western Europe – the metalsmiths found a metal that was easier to work and that could be used to make harder, sharper swords, armor, and agricultural tools. Skilled European smiths produced magnificent objects not only in bronze but in gold and silver too.

*This bronze and gold model from Trundholm is about 2 ft (60 cm) long. It shows the sun being pulled by a horse-drawn chariot.*

## OVERLAND TRADE

These Bronze Age Europeans left no written records, so it is difficult to learn about their trading habits. But metals and prized stones, found far from their places of origin, confirm that the people were active traders. As there was no money, people would have exchanged goods for items they needed. Some goods were carried over amazing distances, which must have increased their value. Amber from the shores of the Baltic Sea was sent overland to southern Europe where Mycenaean merchants bought it and shipped it to the eastern Mediterranean. Tin from England, Spain, France, and Italy was taken overland to central and eastern Europe.

*This cup was carved from a single lump of amber. It was found in a burial mound in Hove, southern England.*

## FOLLOWERS OF FASHION

Ancient garments found in bogs in Denmark give us some idea about what people wore. Clothes, some of which had patterns, were made from wool and linen, while others were made of leather and fur. Men wore tunics, and women dressed in skirts and wool tops. Both sexes wore cloaks. Garments were fastened with buttons of jet, bone, and stone or with metal pins and belts. Some women wore their hair tied back in a bun. Pins that held their hair in place have been found in graves, still in place behind the skulls.

*This magnificent gold collar, which fitted over the shoulders, must have been worn by an important person. It was found around a skeleton in a grave near Mold, in northern Wales.*

19

# MINOANS AND MYCENAEANS

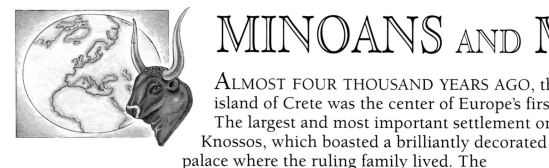

ALMOST FOUR THOUSAND YEARS AGO, the small Mediterranean island of Crete was the center of Europe's first great civilization. The largest and most important settlement on the island was Knossos, which boasted a brilliantly decorated palace where the ruling family lived. The Cretans were great sailors who grew rich by trading with other Mediterranean peoples. They developed their own way of life, which included an extraordinary bull-leaping ceremony. We call these people the Minoans, after a legendary Cretan king named Minos. (A legend is a story, handed down from the past, that may or may not be true.)

The Minoans were very successful. But in about 1450 BC, warriors from mainland Greece took over in Crete. These invaders were Mycenaeans, named after the city where remains of their civilization were first discovered. The Myceaneans lived in small kingdoms on the mainland and seem to have been a warlike people. They adopted many of the Minoan ways of life. Both civilizations spoke an early form of the Greek language and believed in the importance of female gods.

## ISLAND OF PALACES

Archaeologists have discovered the remains of four imposing palaces on Crete – at Knossos, Mallia, Zakro, and Phaistos. The largest, at Knossos, was a huge building, five floors high in places and with 1,300 rooms. The royal rooms were decorated with colorful wall paintings, called frescoes, which showed life at court and sea scenes such as leaping dolphins. The palace complex was built around a central courtyard that was used for religious ceremonies. Knossos had its own water supply and drainage system. Rainwater was channeled into clay pipes that ran through the palace and provided water for the bathrooms and toilets.

*Mycenaean palaces were built on hilltops and protected by high walls made of huge stone blocks. We call these Cyclopean walls, after the one-eyed giant Cyclops, who legend says built the walls.*

*Grapes were used to make wine. They were put in large tubs and trampled on to extract the juice, or wine.*

*Harvesting grain with a sickle*

*Hunting wild boar*

**Iolkos**

**Orchomenos**

**Gla**

**Thebes**

*Minoans and Mycenaeans made intricate gold jewelry like this earring.*

G R E E C E

**Mycenae**

**Athens**

**Tiryns**

*A Mycenaean warrior wore a suit of bronze armor and a helmet decorated with boar's tusks.*

*Early Mycenaean kings were buried in graves protected by a stone circle.*

**Pylos**

I O N I A N

M A N S E A

*This small statue shows the snake goddess, dressed in the Minoan fashion of a flounced skirt and tight bodice, with bare breasts.*

*Women knocked olives from the trees, while men crushed them in a stone press, to extract the oil for cooking and lighting.*

*In about 1450 BC Mycenaeans sailed to Crete and took over the island.*

TRADE ROUTE TO SICILY

M E L

*When archaeologists found the throne room, they discovered the oldest throne in Europe.*

*Bull leaping probably took place in the central courtyard.*

*Cretan townhouses had two or three floors, windows, and a little room on the roof. The outside walls were colorfully painted.*

**Kha**

**Reconstruction of palace at Knossos**

*Light wells allowed daylight and cool air to filter into the palace.*

*The walls were built of local limestone.*

*Wooden pillars were painted in red and blue.*

*Outside the palace grounds, there were groves of olive trees.*

*Legend says that when the Greeks gave up their long siege of Troy, they left behind a huge wooden horse as a gift. When the Trojans brought the horse into their city, Greek warriors hidden inside its hollow body climbed out and opened the gates of Troy. The main army charged in and conquered the city.*

• **Troy**

## THE TROJAN WAR

The legend of the Trojan War is probably based on battles that took place in Mycenaean days. It tells of Paris, Prince of Troy, who eloped with Helen, Queen of Sparta. To get her back from Troy, Helen's husband, Menelaus, and his brother Agamemnon of Mycenae, called all the kings together and set off with a great army. After a siege lasting ten years, the Mycenaeans eventually captured the city using the trick of the wooden horse. Paris and most of the Trojan men were slain, and Helen had to return to her husband, Menelaus.

## GOLDEN MYCENAE

The Mycenaeans lived in hilltop cities such as Tiryns, Gla, and Mycenae itself. At Mycenae, the royal family lived in a beautiful palace on a specially fortified hilltop called a citadel. Anyone who worked for the palace, such as officials, scribes, and craftworkers, lived in the upper town between the palace and the defensive wall. The warrior-kings loved to hunt; they chased lions and stags from their chariots. Most people, however, were farmers or merchants. When the Mycenaeans finally took over Crete, they became the leading traders in the eastern Mediterranean.

When a Mycenaean king died, he was laid out in royal robes, and a gold mask was placed over his face. This mask, once thought to be King Agamemnon's, was found in a grave circle at Mycenae.

A
E
G
E
A
N

S
E
A

A
S
I
A

M
I
N
O
R

*Fishermen caught tuna, mackerel, mullet, and octopus.*

• **Miletus**

*Merchants from the Greek colony of Miletus traded with the Hittites.*

*In about 1450 BC, a volcano erupted on the island of Thera, modern Santorini, and blew the island apart.*

*Mycenaean pottery, ivory, and bronze swords were found on a trading vessel that sank off the coast at Ulu Burun.*

## WRITTEN RECORDS

In Crete and in Mycenaean Greece, the king controlled the economy. Taxes in the form of olive oil, pottery, and metalwork were stored in the palace ready to pay the army, officials, and craftworkers. Any surplus was traded overseas to buy tin, gold, and ivory. Both the Minoans and Mycenaeans kept written records. The Minoans used a form of writing that we call Linear A. The Mycenaeans developed a new script, known as Linear B. So far, experts can only understand Linear B.

M
E
D
I
T
E
R
R
A
N
E
A
N

S
E
A

*Legend says the Minotaur kept in the palace of King Minos was a monster, half man, half bull.*

**Knossos**

**Mallia**

C R E T E

**Zakro**

**Phaistos**

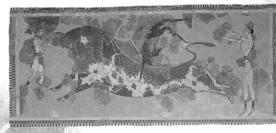

*Oil, grain, and wine were stored in huge pottery jars called pithoi.*

*Young men and women were trained to leap over the backs of charging bulls as part of a religious ceremony. After the ceremony, the bull was sacrificed, and its blood was spread on the land.*

TRADE ROUTE FROM EGYPT

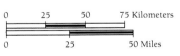
| 0 | 25 | 50 | 75 Kilometers |

| 0 | | 25 | | 50 Miles |

## THE GODDESSES RULE

For both the Minoans and Mycenaeans, the goddess was the most important religious figure. She appeared in many different forms – as a snake goddess, as a goddess of the sea, and as a goddess of caves who looked after women during childbirth. Shrines were built within palaces and in the countryside where people could leave offerings of sweet oils, honey, or wine. Gods only played a secondary role. The Minoans also believed that the bull was a sacred animal; they decorated their palaces and pottery with images of its horns.

Fish, porpoises, and other marine creatures were popular designs on pottery. They show how important the sea was to the Minoans.

# CANAAN – LAND OF PLENTY

CANAAN is the ancient name for the land at the eastern end of the Mediterranean, in what is now Israel and Lebanon, and part of Syria and Jordan. It was to become a land fought over by many people. Around 2000 BC, the countryside boasted huge cedar forests in the north, and good rich soil for farming around the Jordan and Orontes rivers. Canaan also lay at the meeting point between Africa and Asia and was in a perfect position to control trade between the two. Many great empire builders of the day, from the Egyptians to the Mesopotamians, fought for control of this desirable place. Even tribes wandering on the desert fringe dreamed of settling in Canaan's rich farmlands.

Much of what we know about life in Canaan comes from texts written on clay tablets. Tablets found in the city of Ugarit help us understand Canaanite religion. They were written after 1700 BC, when the Canaanites started to use a new way of writing – an alphabet with only 27 letters. This was a breakthrough, as it was much easier to use than the hieroglyphs of Egypt and the cuneiform of Sumer, and formed the basis of the alphabet that we use today.

*Trading ship*

TO MYCENAE

TO EGYPT

*The Egyptians often had to send in their army to keep control of the empire they had won.*

*Hittites, warlike people from what is now Turkey, fought the Egyptians for control of Canaan.*

**Carchemish**

*The Mitanni from northern Mesopotamia added parts of Canaan to their empire for awhile.*

EUPHRATES

**Aleppo**

**Ugarit**

*Rulers of Canaan's many small, rival kingdoms lived in luxurious palaces in well-defended cities.*

ORONTES

*Egyptian pharaoh Tuthmosis III conquered areas as far north as modern-day Syria. For sport, he hunted elephants that roamed the plains.*

**Arvad**

*The tall cedar trees, grown in what is now Lebanon, were exported to nearby people who needed good-quality timber.*

C A N A A N

**Byblos**

*Harvesting wheat and grinding the grain for bread and beer making*

**Tyre**

*Guards kept a close watch over vineyards planted outside the bustling city of Hazor.*

**Hazor**

**Megiddo**

SEA OF GALILEE

*Priests killed sacrificial goats to offer at the "high place" in Megiddo.*

JORDAN

*Nomads grazed their sheep and goats. Some of them became mercenary soldiers; some became bandits.*

**Jericho**

**Jerusalem**

**Lachish**

**Hebron**

*A sturdy watchtower protected the earliest town at Jericho. After surviving many changes, the city was destroyed in about 1560 BC by Egyptians campaigning against the Hyksos people.*

DEAD SEA

M E D I T E R R A N E A N   S E A

| 0 | 25 | 50 | 75 | 100 Kilometers |
|---|----|----|----|----------------|
| 0 | 20 | 40 | 60 | 80 Miles |

This piece of carved ivory from Megiddo shows a Canaanite king with a row of prisoners, probably captured after a battle.

*This strange vase, shaped like a man's head, was found at Jericho. It was made in about 1700 BC.*

## MAKING A LIVING

By 1500 BC, Canaan was a land of city states. Each city and the surrounding farmland and villages was ruled by its own king. Merchants, particularly at the great port of Byblos, took wood, silver, and ivory across the Mediterranean Sea to Egypt and Mycenae in Greece. Artists made fine jewelry and decorated pots. But farmers were the backbone of the community. They kept cows, sheep, and goats and used donkeys for transport.

## WORSHIP IN HIGH PLACES

The chief god in Canaan was El, who ruled the sky. But by far the most popular god was Hadad, better known as Baal, the weather god. His wife, Astarte, was the goddess of love. Gods were served by priests and priestesses in richly decorated temples. They were also worshiped at open-air sites on hilltops, known as "high places," where animals were sacrificed in front of pillars into which priests believed the divine spirits had entered.

This bronze statuette shows the Canaanite god Baal, who usually held a thunderbolt.

## THE CITY OF JERICHO

Jericho is one of the oldest towns in the world. In about 8000 BC, hunters and gatherers settled there because of the reliable supply of food and water. They built houses of mud brick and took up farming. Over the years, they grew rich. They built remarkable stone walls and watchtowers around the town to protect themselves and their wealth. Jericho's wealth may have come from trading salt and bitumen (asphalt) from the Dead Sea.

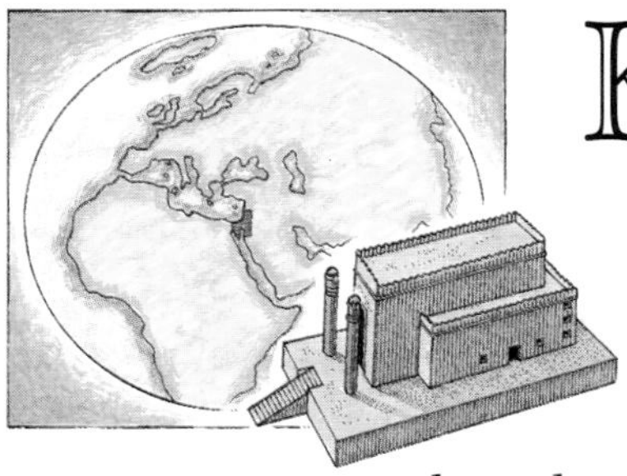

# KINGDOMS OF THE HEBREWS

ACCORDING TO THE BIBLE, the nomadic Hebrew tribes from the land around Canaan were forced to work for the pharaohs in Egypt. They escaped from slavery and returned to conquer Canaan, which they believed had been promised to them by their God. But they had rivals.

Egyptian records show that in about 1200 BC the eastern Mediterranean was threatened by fierce invaders known as the Sea Peoples. One group, the Peleset (from which we get the name Palestine), settled in southern Canaan. In the Bible, the Peleset are called the Philistines.

For almost 200 years, the Philistines and Hebrews lived side by side. But in about 1020 BC the Hebrew tribes united against their old foes and established a strong kingdom known as Israel. The new kingdom prospered under the rule of three great kings, Saul, David, and Solomon. When Solomon died in 922 BC, squabbles between north and south split the kingdom in two, with Israel in the north and Judah in the south. The people of Judah later became known as Jews.

Ancient Jewish texts, now called the Dead Sea Scrolls, were found in 1947 in a cave at Qumran, shown above.

## THE KINGDOM OF SOLOMON
King Solomon reigned from around 960-922 BC and is remembered as a great and wise king. Although it was his father, David, who defeated the Philistines and established Jerusalem as his capital, it was under Solomon that Israel grew rich. He stayed on good terms with his neighbors and even married an Egyptian princess. He kept an army so he could control the major trade routes and collect taxes and payments of gold. The profits were used to build the first temple for the Hebrews.

Once settled, most Hebrews became farmers. They grew wheat and barley, as well as figs, melons, pomegranates, and a variety of nuts.

In 721 BC, Sargon II, king of Assyria, destroyed Samaria, then the capital of Israel.

The Bible tells how a shepherd boy called David killed the Philistine champion, Goliath, with a slingshot.

The Hebrews lived in four-roomed houses. They were sometimes built in a row as a barrier against attack.

The Sea Peoples came from the islands and coasts of the northeast Mediterranean. They were seeking new homes in the Middle East.

The Romans took the hilltop fortress of Masada in AD 74. The defending Jews killed themselves rather than be taken prisoner.

The kingdoms of southern Arabia controlled the incense trade. One Queen of Sabaea (Sheba) is said to have visited King Solomon to test his wisdom.

According to the Bible, the prophet Moses led the Hebrews from Egypt back into Canaan.

Copper from the mines in Sinai was exported from the port of Ezion-Geber.

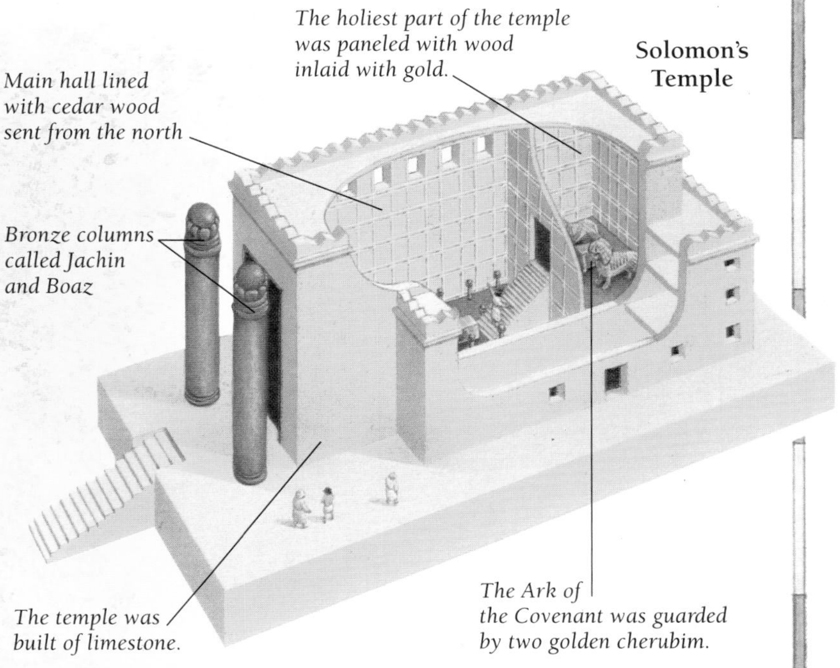

This coin shows the head of King Antiochus IV, whose family, the Seleucids, took Judah from the Greeks. His attacks on the Jewish religion sparked off a revolt led by Judas Maccabaeus in 168 BC.

Trading ship

The holiest part of the temple was paneled with wood inlaid with gold.

**Solomon's Temple**

Main hall lined with cedar wood sent from the north

Bronze columns called Jachin and Boaz

The temple was built of limestone.

The Ark of the Covenant was guarded by two golden cherubim.

## RELIGIOUS TEXTS AND TEMPLES
Among ancient peoples, the Hebrews were unusual because they worshiped only one god, who they called Yahweh. The laws of their religion and the events of their history were gathered into a collection of books, now known to Christians as the Old Testament of the Bible. Solomon built a temple in Jerusalem to house the Ark of the Covenant, a box containing two tablets on which were written the Ten Commandments. The temple became the focus of the religious life of the Hebrews.

## JERUSALEM UNDER SEIGE
The city of Jerusalem was constantly under threat – from Assyrians, Babylonians, Persians, Greeks, and Romans. In 34 BC, the Romans appointed a prince from Edom, Herod the Great, as king. But Herod and his successors were unpopular with their Jewish subjects. Simmering discontent led to several revolts, each savagely suppressed by the Romans, and the majority of the Jews were forced to leave.

0 25 50 75 100 Kilometers
0 20 40 60 80 Miles

# PHOENICIANS – RULERS OF THE SEA

ADVENTUROUS PHOENICIAN SAILORS explored the lands around the Mediterranean Sea. Their magnificent ships carried cedar wood, brightly colored glass, ivory, and purple-dyed cloth to trade with people in faraway lands. By about 700 BC, they had settled colonies on Malta, Sicily, and Sardinia and as far away as Spain. Their most famous trading post was at Carthage in Africa.

The Phoenicians were descended from the Canaanites, who lived along the eastern edge of the Mediterranean Sea. Their main cities were Arvad, Byblos, Berytus (Beirut), Sidon, and Tyre, in modern Lebanon. In about 1200 BC, the area was thrown into chaos by the arrival of the Sea Peoples and by the collapse of the Mycenaean world. The Canaanites were quick to take over as the leading trading nation of the Mediterranean world. In their new role, we call them Phoenicians.

This limestone carving is known as "The Lady of Elche." It was found in Spain, which was part of the Carthaginian Empire.

By 1000 BC, the Phoenicians had produced a simple alphabet. It had 22 letters, which were all consonants. Vowels were added later by the Greeks to form the alphabet we still use today. The Phoenician writing on this stone is from the 4th century BC.

A captain named Himilco sailed around western Spain toward the British Isles. He was probably hoping to open up a sea route to their tin mines.

ATLANTIC OCEAN

TO THE BRITISH ISLES

S P A I N

Spain was rich in minerals. Silver was found in mines around Gades.

After a good catch, fish were dried for future use.

**Gades** (Cadiz)

PILLARS OF HERCULES (STRAITS OF GIBRALTAR)

**Tingis** (Tangiers)

TO WEST AFRICA

In about 425 BC, a captain named Hanno sailed west out of the Mediterranean and headed down the coast of Africa.

A F R I C A

**Ebusus**

BALEARIC ISLANDS

**New Carthage** (Cartagena)

M E D I T E R

Greeks and Phoenicians battled at sea for control of the Mediterranean trade routes.

**Massilia** (Marseille)

CORSICA

SARDINIA

**Caralis** (Cagliari)

**Rome**

The cities of Rome and Carthage became deadly enemies. An army of Carthaginians invaded Italy during the second of the three Punic Wars.

TRADE ROUTE

R A N E A

**Panormus** (Palermo) SICILY

**Carthage**

**Valletta**

MALT

At a special festival in Carthage, sacrifices were offered to the great goddess Tanit

Ships unloaded their goods ready for storage in the warehouses built around the harbor wall.

The harbor at Carthage had workshops for building and repairing ships.

## TRADE NETWORKS

From their great trading cities, the Phoenicians took over the old Mycenaean trading networks. Merchants spread along the north coast of Africa to Spain and then on to the islands of the western Mediterranean. They set up colonies for trading purposes wherever they went. They exported their greatest natural resource – timber from their cedar forests, and cedar oil, together with a variety of manufactured goods. In return they bought copper, silver, and tin for their own use and to sell to other customers.

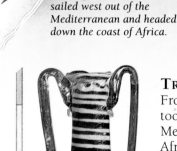

A Phoenician bottle, probably used to hold incense. Glass had already been made by the Egyptians, but it was the Phoenicians who perfected the technique.

## THE CITY OF CARTHAGE

In about 814 BC, colonists from Tyre founded the city of Carthage on the north coast of Africa. Even after the Phoenician homeland was conquered by the Assyrians, Carthage remained an independent power. Its fleets and armies dominated the western Mediterranean. As Rome rose to power, the two cities clashed in three terrible conflicts, known as the Punic Wars. Rome finally won in 146 BC.

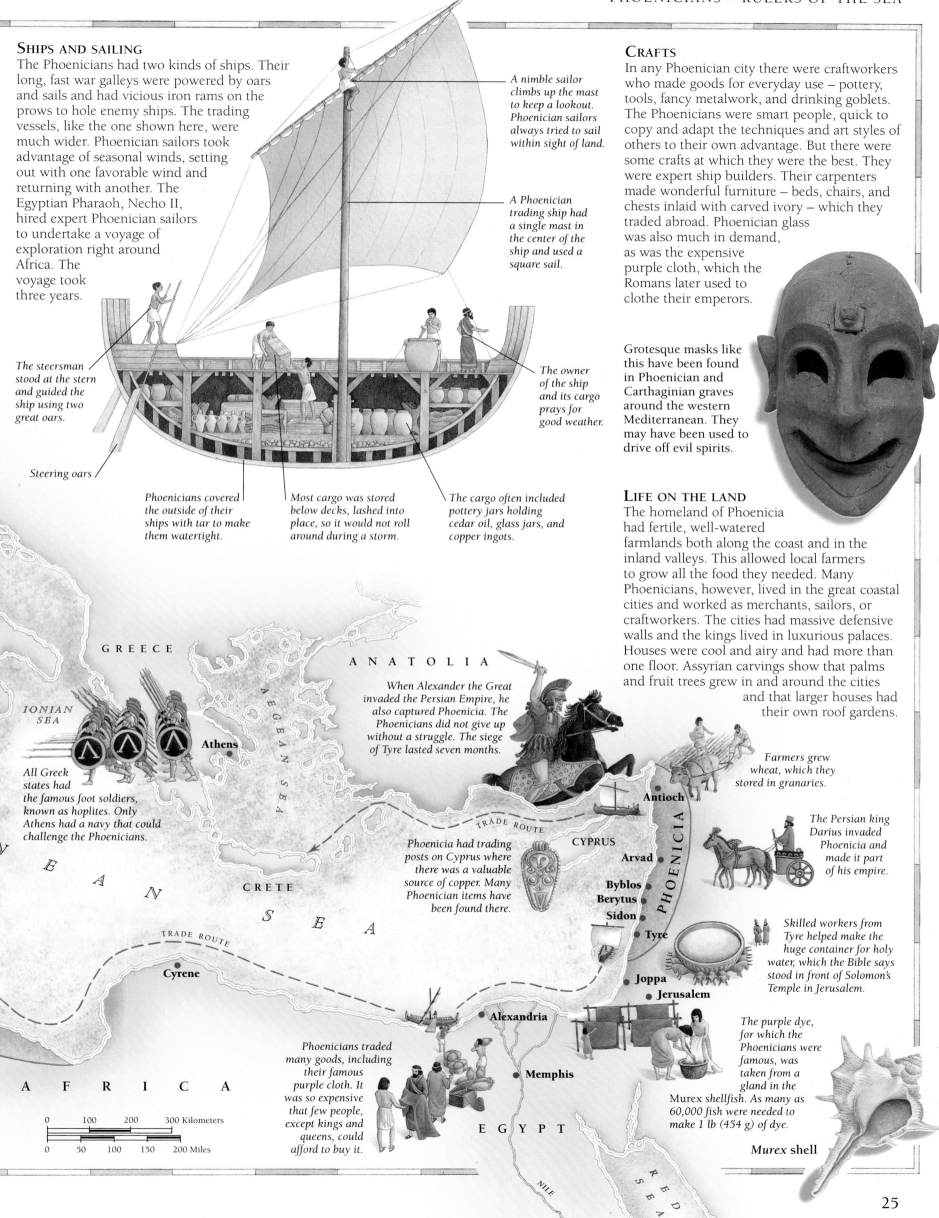

## SHIPS AND SAILING

The Phoenicians had two kinds of ships. Their long, fast war galleys were powered by oars and sails and had vicious iron rams on the prows to hole enemy ships. The trading vessels, like the one shown here, were much wider. Phoenician sailors took advantage of seasonal winds, setting out with one favorable wind and returning with another. The Egyptian Pharaoh, Necho II, hired expert Phoenician sailors to undertake a voyage of exploration right around Africa. The voyage took three years.

A nimble sailor climbs up the mast to keep a lookout. Phoenician sailors always tried to sail within sight of land.

A Phoenician trading ship had a single mast in the center of the ship and used a square sail.

The steersman stood at the stern and guided the ship using two great oars.

Steering oars

The owner of the ship and its cargo prays for good weather.

Phoenicians covered the outside of their ships with tar to make them watertight.

Most cargo was stored below decks, lashed into place, so it would not roll around during a storm.

The cargo often included pottery jars holding cedar oil, glass jars, and copper ingots.

## CRAFTS

In any Phoenician city there were craftworkers who made goods for everyday use – pottery, tools, fancy metalwork, and drinking goblets. The Phoenicians were smart people, quick to copy and adapt the techniques and art styles of others to their own advantage. But there were some crafts at which they were the best. They were expert ship builders. Their carpenters made wonderful furniture – beds, chairs, and chests inlaid with carved ivory – which they traded abroad. Phoenician glass was also much in demand, as was the expensive purple cloth, which the Romans later used to clothe their emperors.

Grotesque masks like this have been found in Phoenician and Carthaginian graves around the western Mediterranean. They may have been used to drive off evil spirits.

## LIFE ON THE LAND

The homeland of Phoenicia had fertile, well-watered farmlands both along the coast and in the inland valleys. This allowed local farmers to grow all the food they needed. Many Phoenicians, however, lived in the great coastal cities and worked as merchants, sailors, or craftworkers. The cities had massive defensive walls and the kings lived in luxurious palaces. Houses were cool and airy and had more than one floor. Assyrian carvings show that palms and fruit trees grew in and around the cities and that larger houses had their own roof gardens.

GREECE

ANATOLIA

When Alexander the Great invaded the Persian Empire, he also captured Phoenicia. The Phoenicians did not give up without a struggle. The siege of Tyre lasted seven months.

IONIAN SEA

AEGEAN SEA

Athens

All Greek states had the famous foot soldiers, known as hoplites. Only Athens had a navy that could challenge the Phoenicians.

CRETE

TRADE ROUTE

Phoenicia had trading posts on Cyprus where there was a valuable source of copper. Many Phoenician items have been found there.

CYPRUS

Antioch

Arvad

Byblos

Berytus

Sidon

Tyre

PHOENICIA

Farmers grew wheat, which they stored in granaries.

The Persian king Darius invaded Phoenicia and made it part of his empire.

Skilled workers from Tyre helped make the huge container for holy water, which the Bible says stood in front of Solomon's Temple in Jerusalem.

TRADE ROUTE

Cyrene

Joppa

Jerusalem

Alexandria

Phoenicians traded many goods, including their famous purple cloth. It was so expensive that few people, except kings and queens, could afford to buy it.

Memphis

EGYPT

AFRICA

| 0 | 100 | 200 | 300 Kilometers |

| 0 | 50 | 100 | 150 | 200 Miles |

The purple dye, for which the Phoenicians were famous, was taken from a gland in the Murex shellfish. As many as 60,000 fish were needed to make 1 lb (454 g) of dye.

**Murex shell**

NILE

RED SEA

# BABYLON – GATE OF THE GODS

BABYLON WAS A MAGNIFICENT CITY. It stood on the banks of the River Euphrates and was protected by walls so wide that two rows of four-horse chariots could ride along the top. The name Babylon means "gate of the gods," and the most impressive way into the city was through the Ishtar Gate. This grand entrance was decorated with brilliant blue tiles and figures of bulls and dragons. Beyond the gate, a wide avenue, called the Processional Way, led to the center of the city and to the temple ziggurat dedicated to the chief god, Marduk. Nearby were the fabulous Hanging Gardens, one of the Seven Wonders of the Ancient World.

*The Hittite army crossed the Taurus Mountains and plundered Babylon around 1595 BC.*

Babylon first became powerful under the rule of King Hammurabi (1792-1750 BC). For many years, it was the capital of Mesopotamia and a center of learning. After hundreds of years of invasions by Kassites, Chaldeans, and Assyrians, Babylon was almost destroyed. It was not until the reign of King Nebuchadnezzar (605-562 BC) that Babylon rose again to become the greatest city of its day.

## HAMMURABI AND THE LAW
In about 1792 BC, a young man named Hammurabi, from an Amorite tribe, inherited the Babylonian throne. Hammurabi conquered all of Sumer and Akkad. We call the new kingdom Babylonia, after its capital city of Babylon. One of his great achievements was to combine the laws of the various parts of his empire. This new code set out laws and penalties covering family, property, slaves, and wages. The idea "an eye for an eye" and "a tooth for a tooth" comes from these ancient law codes.

King Hammurabi's law code was engraved on a stone pillar called a stela. This section shows Hammurabi before Shamash, god of the sun and justice. The stela was carried off by the conquering Persians.

## KASSITES AND CHALDEANS
After Hammurabi's death, people we call Kassites set up a new dynasty in Babylon. They were mountain people, about whom little is known, but they ruled Babylonia successfully from 1595-1155 BC. In about 900 BC, tribesmen known as Chaldeans settled in the coastal marshes of what had been Sumer. They fought for their freedom against the new Assyrian rulers of Babylonia. By 625 BC, Nabopolassar, leader of the Chaldeans, had driven the Assyrians out and become king of Babylonia.

## THE WISE MEN
In Babylon, only boys went to school. They first learned to read and write the 500 or so different signs of their script. Then they went on to study literature, astronomy, and mathematics. Babylonians, like the Sumerians before them, based their mathematics on units of 60. This is where we get our 60 minutes in an hour and 360 degrees in a circle. They also studied the stars and planets and made records of their movements in the sky. Several of the names used by Babylonian astronomers, such as the Twins (Gemini), the Scorpion, and Capricorn, are still used to describe constellations today.

This clay tablet shows a map of the world as the Babylonians saw it. The outer circle is marked as the ocean, with the known world at the center.

*This glazed head of a Kassite priestess comes from a tomb in Ur.*

## THE MISSING KING
King Nabonidus (556-539 BC) was the last king of Babylonia – and a bit of a mystery. He was devoted to the moon god, Sin, and restored many temples. However, he was unpopular because he could not solve the economic problems left by earlier kings. Suddenly, without warning, he moved to the oasis of Tayma in the Arabian desert, leaving his son Belshazzar in charge. He stayed away for ten years. No one knows why. By the time he returned, the Persian king, Cyrus the Great, had captured Babylon.

*In 597 BC, King Jehoiachin and 10,000 leading citizens of Jerusalem were carried off into captivity in Babylon.*

TAURUS

MEDITERRANEAN SEA

Ebl

Byblos

Damascus

Tyre

JORDAN

Samaria

ISRAEL

Jerusalem

JUDAH

DEAD SEA

RED SEA

| | 50 | 100 | 150 Kilometers |
| 0 | 100 | 200 | 300 Miles |

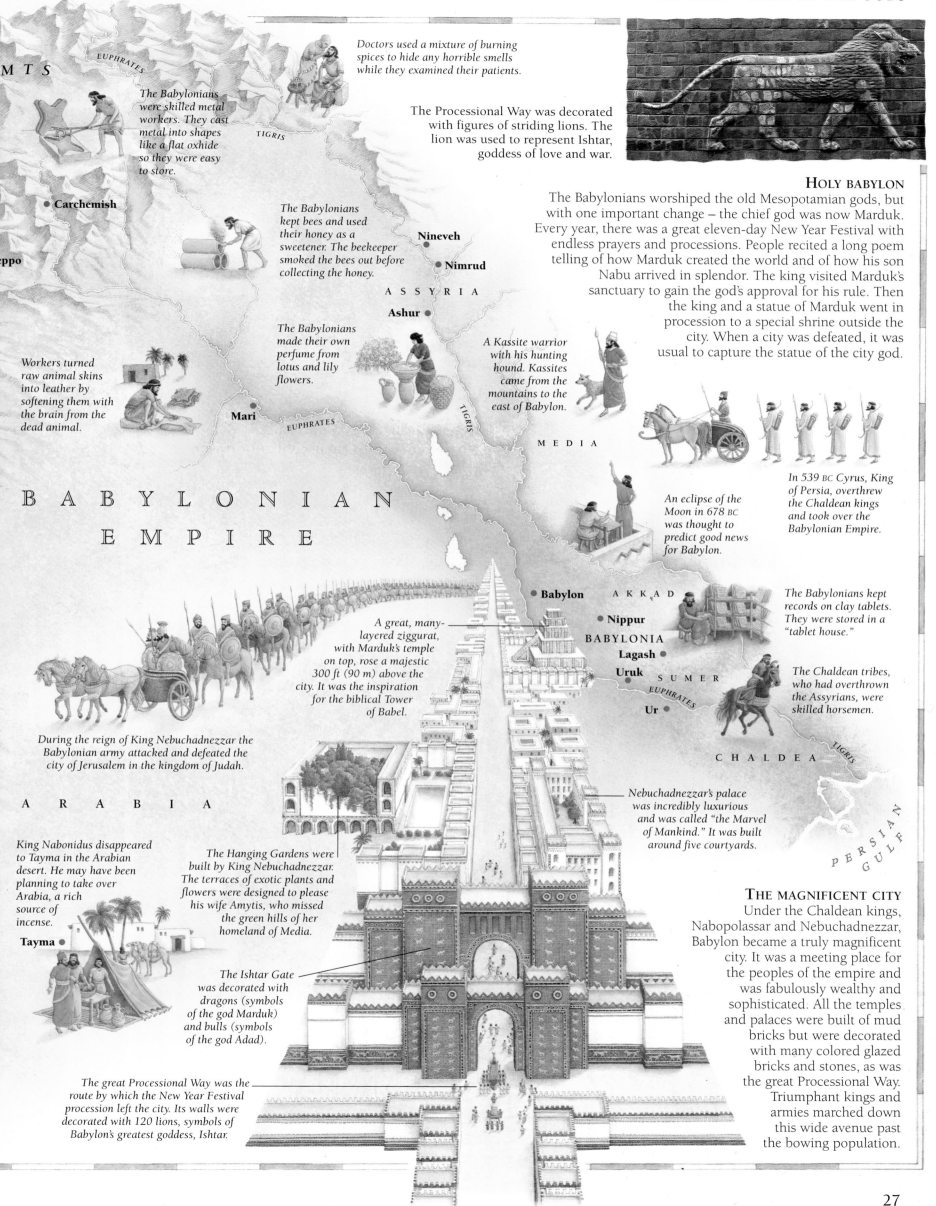

The Babylonians were skilled metal workers. They cast metal into shapes like a flat oxhide so they were easy to store.

Doctors used a mixture of burning spices to hide any horrible smells while they examined their patients.

The Processional Way was decorated with figures of striding lions. The lion was used to represent Ishtar, goddess of love and war.

**Carchemish**

**eppo**

The Babylonians kept bees and used their honey as a sweetener. The beekeeper smoked the bees out before collecting the honey.

**Nineveh**

**Nimrud**

A S S Y R I A

**Ashur**

### HOLY BABYLON
The Babylonians worshiped the old Mesopotamian gods, but with one important change – the chief god was now Marduk. Every year, there was a great eleven-day New Year Festival with endless prayers and processions. People recited a long poem telling of how Marduk created the world and of how his son Nabu arrived in splendor. The king visited Marduk's sanctuary to gain the god's approval for his rule. Then the king and a statue of Marduk went in procession to a special shrine outside the city. When a city was defeated, it was usual to capture the statue of the city god.

Workers turned raw animal skins into leather by softening them with the brain from the dead animal.

The Babylonians made their own perfume from lotus and lily flowers.

**Mari**

EUPHRATES

A Kassite warrior with his hunting hound. Kassites came from the mountains to the east of Babylon.

M E D I A

An eclipse of the Moon in 678 BC was thought to predict good news for Babylon.

In 539 BC Cyrus, King of Persia, overthrew the Chaldean kings and took over the Babylonian Empire.

# B A B Y L O N I A N
# E M P I R E

A great, many-layered ziggurat, with Marduk's temple on top, rose a majestic 300 ft (90 m) above the city. It was the inspiration for the biblical Tower of Babel.

**Babylon**

A K K A D

**Nippur**

B A B Y L O N I A

**Lagash**

**Uruk**

S U M E R

**Ur**

EUPHRATES

C H A L D E A

The Babylonians kept records on clay tablets. They were stored in a "tablet house."

The Chaldean tribes, who had overthrown the Assyrians, were skilled horsemen.

During the reign of King Nebuchadnezzar the Babylonian army attacked and defeated the city of Jerusalem in the kingdom of Judah.

A R A B I A

Nebuchadnezzar's palace was incredibly luxurious and was called "the Marvel of Mankind." It was built around five courtyards.

King Nabonidus disappeared to Tayma in the Arabian desert. He may have been planning to take over Arabia, a rich source of incense.

**Tayma**

The Hanging Gardens were built by King Nebuchadnezzar. The terraces of exotic plants and flowers were designed to please his wife Amytis, who missed the green hills of her homeland of Media.

The Ishtar Gate was decorated with dragons (symbols of the god Marduk) and bulls (symbols of the god Adad).

P E R S I A N   G U L F

### THE MAGNIFICENT CITY
Under the Chaldean kings, Nabopolassar and Nebuchadnezzar, Babylon became a truly magnificent city. It was a meeting place for the peoples of the empire and was fabulously wealthy and sophisticated. All the temples and palaces were built of mud bricks but were decorated with many colored glazed bricks and stones, as was the great Processional Way. Triumphant kings and armies marched down this wide avenue past the bowing population.

The great Processional Way was the route by which the New Year Festival procession left the city. Its walls were decorated with 120 lions, symbols of Babylon's greatest goddess, Ishtar.

# ASSYRIANS – KINGS OF CONQUEST

THE ASSYRIANS had to fight to survive. They originally lived in the rolling hills around the Tigris River, in what is now northern Iraq, but they were surrounded by people who wanted their land. Until about 2000 BC, the kings of Sumer and Akkad controlled Assyria. Finally it was taken over by invaders from the southwest, who gave them independence. Over the years, the Assyrians tried to extend their land, but they were always beaten back. Then, in the 9th century BC, came triumph. Under orders from the chief god Ashur, the Assyrian kings began to conquer the surrounding kingdoms. They achieved this without any thought for human life and property. Defeated people were marched off to labor as slaves on building projects or in the households of their conquerors. By 612 BC, the empire was too large to control and was defeated by an army of Babylonians and Medes.

### POWER OF THE KINGS

The Assyrian kings had grand titles like "Great King," and "King of the Universe." The kings believed they were chosen by the gods to bring wealth to the land. As the representative of god on earth, the king was in charge of his subjects. But he also had to serve the gods. He was responsible for the priests and the temples and took the lead in great religious events. At one ceremony, the high priest had to slap the king to remind him he was only a servant of the gods.

This statue is of King Ashurnasirpal II (883-859 BC) who built the palace at Nimrud. The king holds a mace, the symbol of authority.

The map shows the full extent of the Assyrian empire. Years of almost nonstop war built up an empire that stretched all the way from the Persian Gulf to Egypt.

### LIFE AT COURT

The Assyrians built beautiful cities. Their earliest capital was at Ashur, named after the god. Later kings preferred other cities. King Sennacherib (704-681 BC) made Nineveh his headquarters. The palace was decorated with glazed tiles and great stone carvings telling of the king's conquests. Inside there were at least 80 large, cool rooms, including a throne room and a library. Some kings even had a special park where they kept lions, leopards, bears, and elephants.

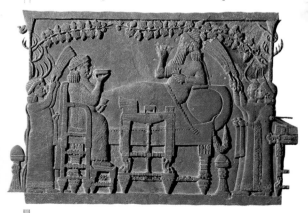

King Ashurbanipal (668-627 BC) relaxes with Queen Ashursharrat at Nineveh. They are celebrating victory over the Elamites.

Stone carvings showing famous battles decorated the palace walls. This scene shows the army attacking a town in Egypt.

Native princes ruled in Egypt, but Assyrian officials kept an eye on them.

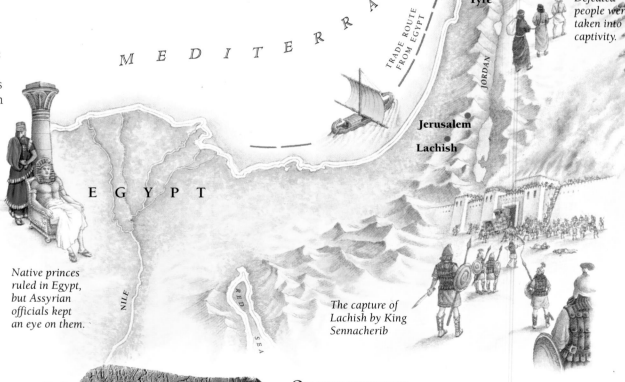

Wood from the tall cedar trees of Lebanon was used for building boats.

Defeated people were taken into captivity.

The capture of Lachish by King Sennacherib

### ON THE WARPATH

Military campaigns were planned in detail, with the king often leading his men into battle. Most of the army was made up of foot soldiers who did the dangerous fighting. They used bows, swords, slings, spears, and battle-axes, and carried shields to protect themselves. When the army came home after a successful battle, there was a grand procession through the city to the temple, where the king reported the good news to the god.

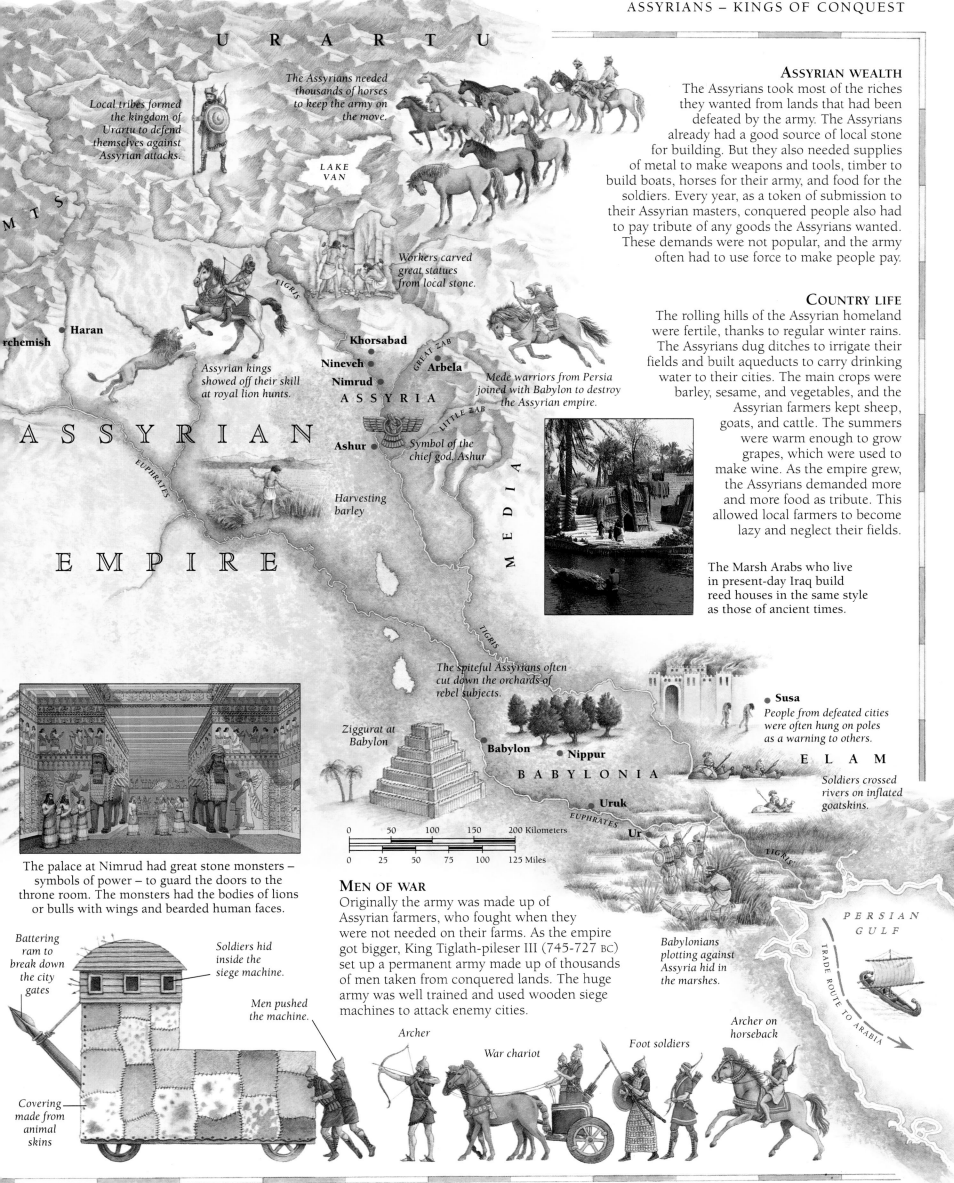

U R A R T U

*Local tribes formed the kingdom of Urartu to defend themselves against Assyrian attacks.*

*The Assyrians needed thousands of horses to keep the army on the move.*

LAKE VAN

## ASSYRIAN WEALTH

The Assyrians took most of the riches they wanted from lands that had been defeated by the army. The Assyrians already had a good source of local stone for building. But they also needed supplies of metal to make weapons and tools, timber to build boats, horses for their army, and food for the soldiers. Every year, as a token of submission to their Assyrian masters, conquered people also had to pay tribute of any goods the Assyrians wanted. These demands were not popular, and the army often had to use force to make people pay.

M T S

TIGRIS

*Workers carved great statues from local stone.*

rchemish  ● Haran

*Assyrian kings showed off their skill at royal lion hunts.*

● **Khorsabad**

GREAT ZAB

**Nineveh** ●

● **Arbela**

**Nimrud** ●

A S S Y R I A

*Mede warriors from Persia joined with Babylon to destroy the Assyrian empire.*

LITTLE ZAB

EUPHRATES

**Ashur** ●  *Symbol of the chief god, Ashur.*

M E D I A

*Harvesting barley*

## COUNTRY LIFE

The rolling hills of the Assyrian homeland were fertile, thanks to regular winter rains. The Assyrians dug ditches to irrigate their fields and built aqueducts to carry drinking water to their cities. The main crops were barley, sesame, and vegetables, and the Assyrian farmers kept sheep, goats, and cattle. The summers were warm enough to grow grapes, which were used to make wine. As the empire grew, the Assyrians demanded more and more food as tribute. This allowed local farmers to become lazy and neglect their fields.

A S S Y R I A N

E M P I R E

*The Marsh Arabs who live in present-day Iraq build reed houses in the same style as those of ancient times.*

TIGRIS

*The spiteful Assyrians often cut down the orchards of rebel subjects.*

● **Susa**

*People from defeated cities were often hung on poles as a warning to others.*

*Ziggurat at Babylon*

E L A M

**Babylon** ● ● **Nippur**

B A B Y L O N I A

*Soldiers crossed rivers on inflated goatskins.*

● **Uruk**

EUPHRATES

● **Ur**

TIGRIS

*The palace at Nimrud had great stone monsters – symbols of power – to guard the doors to the throne room. The monsters had the bodies of lions or bulls with wings and bearded human faces.*

| 0 | 50 | 100 | 150 | 200 Kilometers |
|---|----|-----|-----|----------------|

| 0 | 25 | 50 | 75 | 100 | 125 Miles |
|---|----|----|----|-----|-----------|

*Babylonians plotting against Assyria hid in the marshes.*

P E R S I A N
G U L F

TRADE ROUTE TO ARABIA

## MEN OF WAR

Originally the army was made up of Assyrian farmers, who fought when they were not needed on their farms. As the empire got bigger, King Tiglath-pileser III (745-727 BC) set up a permanent army made up of thousands of men taken from conquered lands. The huge army was well trained and used wooden siege machines to attack enemy cities.

*Battering ram to break down the city gates*

*Soldiers hid inside the siege machine.*

*Men pushed the machine.*

*Covering made from animal skins*

*Archer*

*War chariot*

*Foot soldiers*

*Archer on horseback*

# CELTS – IRON AGE HEROES

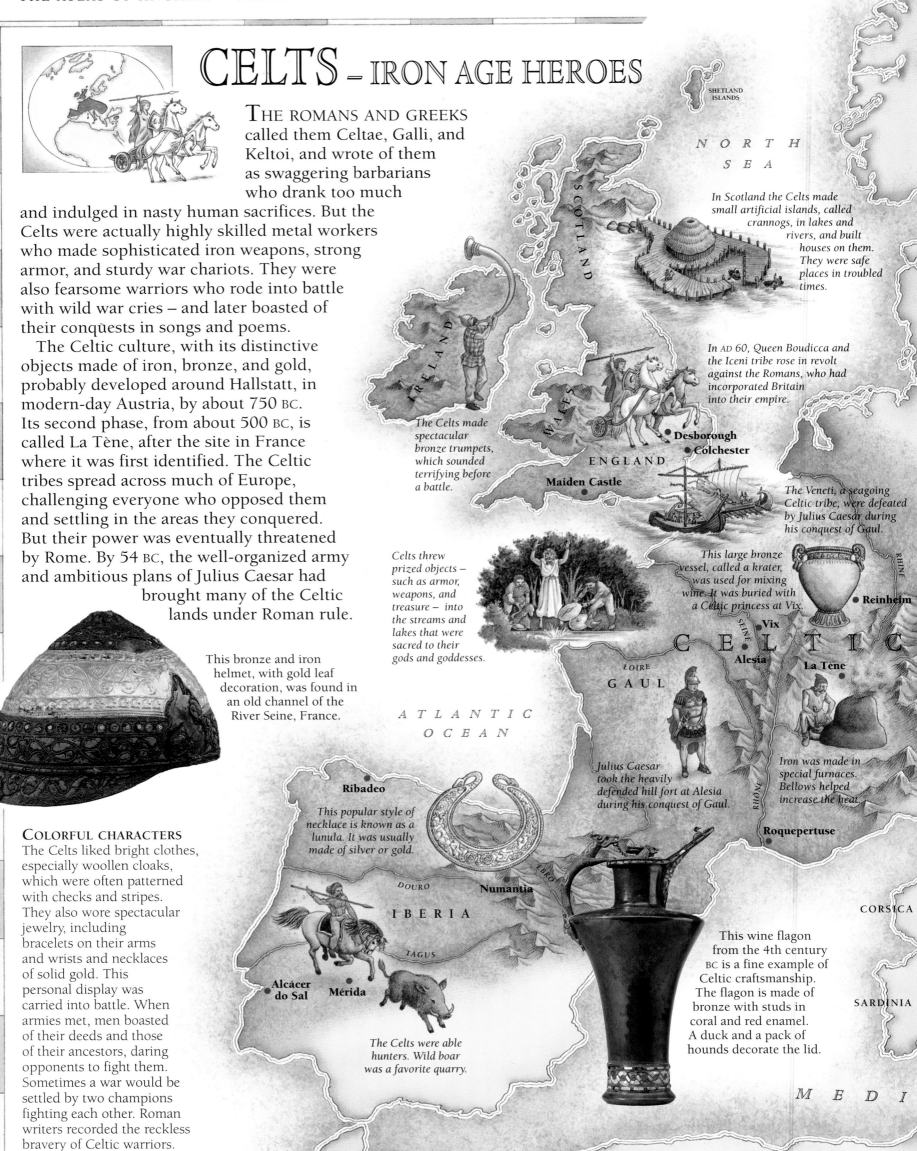

THE ROMANS AND GREEKS called them Celtae, Galli, and Keltoi, and wrote of them as swaggering barbarians who drank too much and indulged in nasty human sacrifices. But the Celts were actually highly skilled metal workers who made sophisticated iron weapons, strong armor, and sturdy war chariots. They were also fearsome warriors who rode into battle with wild war cries – and later boasted of their conquests in songs and poems.

The Celtic culture, with its distinctive objects made of iron, bronze, and gold, probably developed around Hallstatt, in modern-day Austria, by about 750 BC. Its second phase, from about 500 BC, is called La Tène, after the site in France where it was first identified. The Celtic tribes spread across much of Europe, challenging everyone who opposed them and settling in the areas they conquered. But their power was eventually threatened by Rome. By 54 BC, the well-organized army and ambitious plans of Julius Caesar had brought many of the Celtic lands under Roman rule.

This bronze and iron helmet, with gold leaf decoration, was found in an old channel of the River Seine, France.

## COLORFUL CHARACTERS

The Celts liked bright clothes, especially woollen cloaks, which were often patterned with checks and stripes. They also wore spectacular jewelry, including bracelets on their arms and wrists and necklaces of solid gold. This personal display was carried into battle. When armies met, men boasted of their deeds and those of their ancestors, daring opponents to fight them. Sometimes a war would be settled by two champions fighting each other. Roman writers recorded the reckless bravery of Celtic warriors.

In Scotland the Celts made small artificial islands, called crannogs, in lakes and rivers, and built houses on them. They were safe places in troubled times.

In AD 60, Queen Boudicca and the Iceni tribe rose in revolt against the Romans, who had incorporated Britain into their empire.

The Celts made spectacular bronze trumpets, which sounded terrifying before a battle.

The Veneti, a seagoing Celtic tribe, were defeated by Julius Caesar during his conquest of Gaul.

This large bronze vessel, called a krater, was used for mixing wine. It was buried with a Celtic princess at Vix.

Celts threw prized objects – such as armor, weapons, and treasure – into the streams and lakes that were sacred to their gods and goddesses.

Julius Caesar took the heavily defended hill fort at Alesia during his conquest of Gaul.

Iron was made in special furnaces. Bellows helped increase the heat.

This popular style of necklace is known as a lunula. It was usually made of silver or gold.

The Celts were able hunters. Wild boar was a favorite quarry.

This wine flagon from the 4th century BC is a fine example of Celtic craftsmanship. The flagon is made of bronze with studs in coral and red enamel. A duck and a pack of hounds decorate the lid.

SHETLAND ISLANDS

NORTH SEA

SCOTLAND

IRELAND

WALES

ENGLAND

Desborough

Colchester

Maiden Castle

RHINE

Reinheim

SEINE

Vix

CELTIC

Alesia

La Tène

GAUL

LOIRE

ATLANTIC OCEAN

RHONE

Roquepertuse

Ribadeo

DOURO

IBERIA

Numantia

EBRO

TAGUS

Alcácer do Sal

Mérida

CORSICA

SARDINIA

MEDI

AFRICA

## DAILY LIFE

The people of Celtic Europe were organized into tribes of varying sizes, led by chieftains. Women had rights and were treated with respect, and the sick and the old were well cared for. Most people were farmers living in small villages, but just before the Romans arrived in Britain and Gaul, some Celts began to live in larger settlements that might be called towns. Houses were built of wood or stone, according to what was available locally. They also built roads paved with wooden beams.

*The tribes the Romans called Germani lived east of the River Rhine.*

*The skull of an enemy was often placed over the door.*

*A scene inside a typical Celtic home*

*The frame of the house was made of wooden posts, and the roof was thatch, or straw.*

*Women cooked meals in a great iron cauldron that hung from a crossbeam by a long chain.*

*The walls were made of carefully woven branches plastered with clay. This is called wattle and daub.*

*Before a battle, warriors in Britain painted blue patterns on their bodies.*

*Men often shaved their cheeks but kept a long mustache.*

*Children played a game with a ball and a stick, much like hockey.*

## SKULLS AND SACRIFICES

The Celts had many gods and goddesses to care for them in this world and the next. They sacrificed valuable objects to their gods – and sometimes people, too. Roman writers said the Celts believed their souls would go to the next world, rest awhile, and then be reborn on earth. They believed their souls were in their heads, saving the skulls of honored ancestors or great enemies. The religious leaders of the Celts were known as druids.

Magnificent bronze mirrors, like this one found at Desborough, England, were status symbols. They showed off the skill of Celtic artists.

Human skulls were displayed in stone shrines like these found at Roquepertuse in southern France.

## FEASTS AND FESTIVALS

The Celts celebrated many festivals with grand feasts, songs, and games. Wine was often drunk, but the most popular drink was beer made from rye or wheat. The Celts loved music. Poet-musicians called bards learned long poems by heart about heroes and their deeds. They sang them at their chieftain's feasts, accompanying themselves on harps. They also wrote songs that poked fun at some of their chief's enemies.

## FORTS AND FIGHTS

To protect themselves, the Celts built fortresses on hilltops, and surrounded them with huge earth walls and wooden palisades. Wars between tribes were common, so the hill forts offered safety to people and their treasure. Brave Celtic warriors often fought as individual heroes, not as an organized unit. They did not even join forces to fight the disciplined units of the Roman army. Only in Ireland and northern Scotland did the Celts escape conquest by Rome.

*The Celts were efficient farmers. They used a special reaping machine to harvest the grain.*

*At Hallstatt the Celts controlled large salt mines which made them wealthy.*

*A chieftain, his wife, and child dressed up for a festival.*

*Celts known as Galli migrated eastward. They settled in an area of Asia Minor named Galatia.*

*The Celts invaded Rome in 387 BC. One area was saved from a surprise attack when geese cackled so loudly they raised the alarm.*

*In 279 BC, one group of migrating Celts invaded Greece and sacked the shrine of the god Apollo at Delphi.*

*Many Gauls killed themselves and their families after being defeated by Attolos I of Pergamum in 241 BC.*

SCANDINAVIA

GERMANY

DANUBE

EUROPE

Hallein (Salzburg)   Hallstatt

TIBER

ADRIATIC SEA

Rome

ITALY

SICILY

MEDITERRANEAN SEA

GREECE

Delphi

CRETE

DANUBE

BLACK SEA

Ancyra (Ankara)

GALATIA

ASIA MINOR

Pergamum

CYPRUS

| 0 | 100 | 200 | 300 Kilometers |
| 0 | 50 | 100 | 150 | 200 Miles |

# PERSIA – THE MAGNIFICENT EMPIRE

IN JUST 30 YEARS, the Persians grew from being a minor tribe on the fringes of Babylon to ruling the most powerful nation in the world. The Persians, and their neighbors the Medes, first moved into modern-day Iran in about 1300 BC. For many years, the Medes ruled the area. Then, in 549 BC, Cyrus became king of the Persians. With great daring, he took over the kingdom of Media, even though the king was his own grandfather. He defeated the Greek colonies in Ionia and conquered the kingdom of Lydia, with its rich resources of gold. Finally, in 539 BC, he seized the mighty Babylonian Empire.

For more than 200 years, the kings of Persia ruled supreme. The Persians were skilled warriors, horse riders, and craftworkers. They were also highly organized. To control the vast empire, which now stretched from Egypt to India, King Darius I (522-486 BC) divided the land into provinces, called satrapies. Sturdy roads linked the farthest corners of the empire, and tribute and taxes poured into the palaces at Persepolis and Susa.

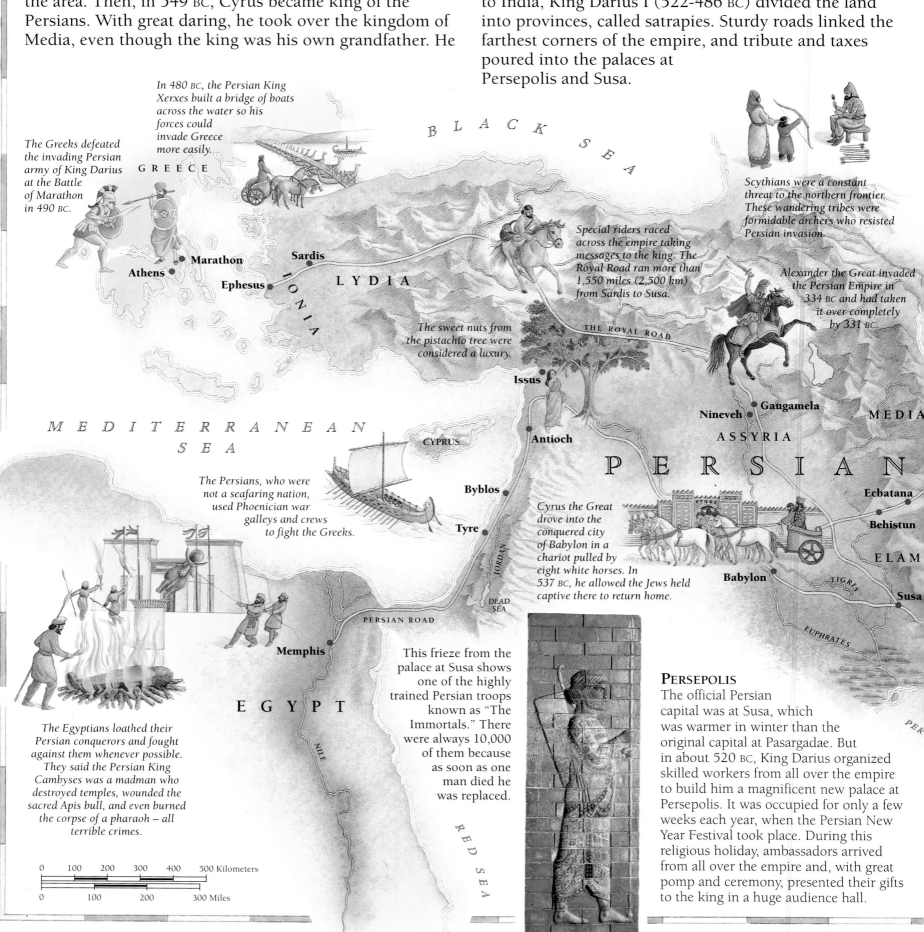

*In 480 BC, the Persian King Xerxes built a bridge of boats across the water so his forces could invade Greece more easily.*

*The Greeks defeated the invading Persian army of King Darius at the Battle of Marathon in 490 BC.*

*Scythians were a constant threat to the northern frontier. These wandering tribes were formidable archers who resisted Persian invasion.*

*Special riders raced across the empire taking messages to the king. The Royal Road ran more than 1,550 miles (2,500 km) from Sardis to Susa.*

*Alexander the Great invaded the Persian Empire in 334 BC and had taken it over completely by 331 BC.*

*The sweet nuts from the pistachio tree were considered a luxury.*

*The Persians, who were not a seafaring nation, used Phoenician war galleys and crews to fight the Greeks.*

*Cyrus the Great drove into the conquered city of Babylon in a chariot pulled by eight white horses. In 537 BC, he allowed the Jews held captive there to return home.*

*The Egyptians loathed their Persian conquerors and fought against them whenever possible. They said the Persian King Cambyses was a madman who destroyed temples, wounded the sacred Apis bull, and even burned the corpse of a pharaoh – all terrible crimes.*

This frieze from the palace at Susa shows one of the highly trained Persian troops known as "The Immortals." There were always 10,000 of them because as soon as one man died he was replaced.

GREECE · Athens · Marathon · Sardis · Ephesus · IONIA · LYDIA · BLACK SEA · Issus · Nineveh · Gaugamela · MEDIA · ASSYRIA · Antioch · CYPRUS · P E R S I A N · Ecbatana · Behistun · ELAM · Babylon · Susa · MEDITERRANEAN SEA · Byblos · Tyre · JORDAN · DEAD SEA · PERSIAN ROAD · Memphis · EGYPT · NILE · RED SEA · TIGRIS · EUPHRATES · THE ROYAL ROAD

### PERSEPOLIS
The official Persian capital was at Susa, which was warmer in winter than the original capital at Pasargadae. But in about 520 BC, King Darius organized skilled workers from all over the empire to build him a magnificent new palace at Persepolis. It was occupied for only a few weeks each year, when the Persian New Year Festival took place. During this religious holiday, ambassadors arrived from all over the empire and, with great pomp and ceremony, presented their gifts to the king in a huge audience hall.

| 0 | 100 | 200 | 300 | 400 | 500 Kilometers |

| 0 | 100 | 200 | 300 Miles |

## THE KING OF KINGS

The Persian monarchs claimed the title "King of Kings" to show their total power over other rulers. The king had supreme power; everywhere he went, he was surrounded by courtiers and officials chosen from the noblest families. He also had many wives who lived together in a special household called a harem. But people were jealous and constantly plotted to murder the king. To avoid coming to a sticky end, kings often had their male relatives killed just in case they posed a threat.

This model shows a four-horse Persian chariot with a charioteer and a passenger. It is made of gold and was part of the Oxus Treasure.

## THE KING'S EARS

The Persian Empire was so vast that it was divided into 20 provinces, called satrapies. Each satrapy was ruled by a governor, or satrap, acting on behalf of the king. But the king had to check whether his officials were really as loyal as they claimed. He needed to know if they were collecting the correct amount of tax or if they were taking more and pocketing the extra. So he could be kept informed about his officials, the king had special servants, known as "The King's Ears," who listened for the slightest hint of treachery.

## THE GREEK WARS

There was no love lost between the Greeks and the Persians. When the Greek colonies in Ionia lost their independence to the Persians, the armies of mainland Greece came to their aid. This sparked off a series of Persian attacks. King Darius I and King Xerxes invaded Greece in 490 and 480 BC, respectively. The Greeks were outnumbered and suffered several setbacks, but they eventually defeated each invasion, with victories on land and sea. The wars left the Greeks with a hatred of Persians and a desire for revenge, which they finally achieved under Alexander the Great.

This mosaic shows the Persian King Darius III fleeing from Alexander during the Battle of Issus in 333 BC.

The Massagetae were nomads who withstood Persian attempts to conquer them. King Cyrus died during a campaign against them.

This silver drinking vessel, called a rhyton, was made around 400 BC. The griffin at the base of the vessel was an imaginary creature that often appeared in Persian decoration.

This gold armlet is part of the Oxus Treasure found near the Oxus River, in the province of Bactria (part of modern Afghanistan).

Caravans of two-humped Bactrian camels carried silver, spices, and ivory across the empire.

**BACTRIA**

**Bactra**

PERSIAN ROAD

**Kabul**

**Taxila**

**Alexandria Areion** (Herat)

The satrap of an Indian province watched his staff as they weighed out gold to be taken to the King of Persia.

The palace at Persepolis had high-columned audience halls, store rooms for tribute, and barracks for the army.

**INDIA**

## SO SPEAKS ZARATHUSTRA

The Persians worshiped many deities. Then, in about 600 BC, a prophet named Zarathustra (also called Zoroaster) preached of a supreme god of goodness, light, and truth, named Ahura Mazda, the Wise Lord. But there were also evil, darkness, and lies in the world. People had to choose which to follow and, when they died, they would be rewarded or punished according to the life they had led. Fire played an important part in the Zoroastrian religion and was thought to represent the truth of the Wise Lord. The priests of the new faith were called Magi, from which we get our word "magic."

Priests looked after the altar bearing the sacred fire of Zoroastrianism, a religion that is still practiced today.

**Pasargadae**

**Persepolis**

The King of Kings sat in state on his throne and received tribute from all parts of his empire. This scene was carved along the stone stairway leading to the main audience hall at Persepolis.

Assyrian bringing a pony

Indian carrying pots of gold dust

Babylonian leading a prize bull

Elamite offering a young lion

# GREECE – THE POWER AND THE GLORY

By ABOUT 800 BC, a glorious new culture had begun to emerge on the Greek mainland. Now the Greeks were inspired to produce fine art and great buildings; they also studied music and wrote plays, puzzled over mathematics and medicine, and discussed political ideas. They introduced a system of government in which men had a say in how their city state was run. Many of the words that we use in English come from the language spoken by the ancient Greeks.

But Greece was not a united country. The hot, often mountainous, mainland and islands were divided into many small city states, each with its own surrounding farmlands and villages. The most powerful city state was Athens, which became the center of Greek civilization and culture in the 5th century BC. It had a well-trained army and the most powerful navy in the ancient world.

## POWER TO THE PEOPLE

Each of the city states in Greece was called a *polis*, from which we get our word "politics." By about 510 BC, most states had gotten rid of their kings. They preferred to be ruled by a small group of leaders (known as an oligarchy) or by one powerful politician (called a tyrant). In 508 BC, Athens introduced the idea of democracy, meaning "rule by the people." This gave ordinary men a chance to help make decisions. Male citizens decided on the law by voting at a special meeting called the Assembly. Women, foreigners, and slaves were not allowed to vote.

The Athenians chose the powerful politician, Pericles, to lead them from 443 to 429 BC. He organized building the temples on the Acropolis.

## THE GREEK COLONIES

The population of the city states grew so rapidly that, between 750-550 BC, many people were forced to seek new homes overseas. They spread around the Black Sea and to those parts of the Mediterranean where their rivals, the Phoenicians, had not already set up colonies. Once settled, they farmed and built cities in the Greek style, introducing their own way of life and culture. They also established profitable trading links with their homeland.

*A Macedonian shepherd and his flock. The Greeks thought the Macedonians were a backward people and not true Greeks.*

*Greek decorated pottery was of high quality. The black and red wares were made from special clay that turned red when fired.*

*In Greek religion, Mount Olympus was the home of the gods and goddesses.*

*In a democracy, politicians had to be good public speakers in order to influence their fellow citizens.*

*Good pasture land in Thessaly made it perfect for horse breeding.*

AEGEAN SEA

*Money, invented in Lydia, was soon used by the Greeks. This coin from Athens is stamped with the goddess Athene's owl.*

*The Greeks visited the oracle at Delphi to ask the gods about the future.*

*The Olympic Games were first held in 776 BC as part of a festival to honor the god Zeus.*

*Athens and Sparta were deadly rivals.*

*Athens controlled one of the few sources of precious metal in Greece, the silver mines in Laurion.*

MACEDONIA — Pella, Thessalonica

KERKYRA (CORFU)

EPIRUS

Ambracia

IONIAN SEA

THESSALY — Thermopylae, Delphi, Plataea

PELOPONNESE — Corinth, Olympia, Marathon, ATTICA, Eleusis, Athens, Piraeus, SALAMIS, ANDROS, AEGINA

MESSENIA — Sparta

*Spartans who did not show enough courage were forced to grow half a beard. People would then tease and humiliate them.*

*Greek women wove most of the cloth used for household linen, wall hangings, and clothes for their family.*

MEDI

Cydonia

CR

GAUL — EUROPE — Massilia, Nicaea, ITALY, Cumae, MAGNA GRAECIA, SICILY, Syracuse, IBERIA, Odessus, BLACK SEA, Byzantium, Chalcedon, GREECE, LYDIA, IONIA, Ephesus, Athens, ASIA, MEDITERRANEAN SEA, AFRICA, Cyrene, Naucratis, EGYPT, Sidon, Tyre, PHOENICIA

The shaded parts of the map on the left show Greece and the main areas settled by Greek colonists during 750-550 BC.

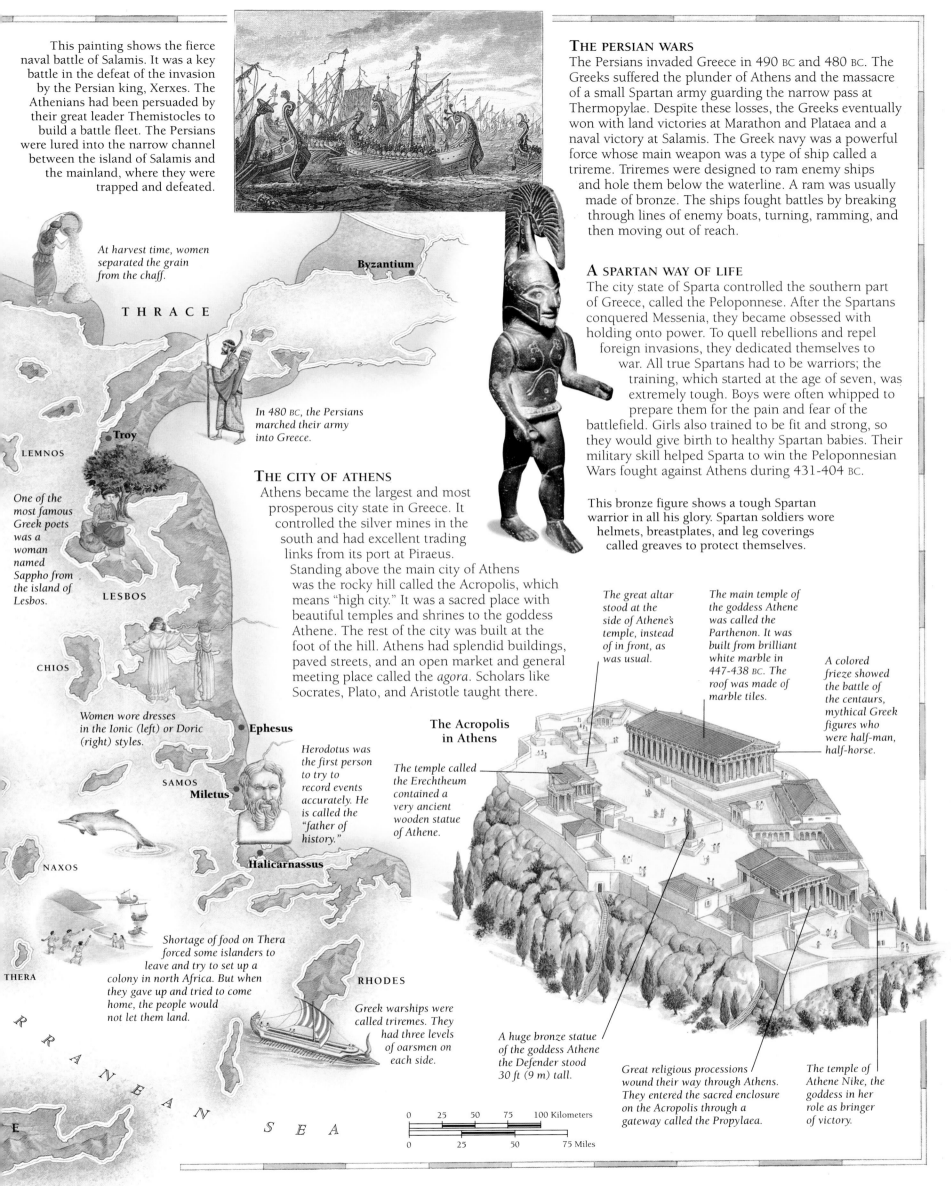

This painting shows the fierce naval battle of Salamis. It was a key battle in the defeat of the invasion by the Persian king, Xerxes. The Athenians had been persuaded by their great leader Themistocles to build a battle fleet. The Persians were lured into the narrow channel between the island of Salamis and the mainland, where they were trapped and defeated.

## THE PERSIAN WARS

The Persians invaded Greece in 490 BC and 480 BC. The Greeks suffered the plunder of Athens and the massacre of a small Spartan army guarding the narrow pass at Thermopylae. Despite these losses, the Greeks eventually won with land victories at Marathon and Plataea and a naval victory at Salamis. The Greek navy was a powerful force whose main weapon was a type of ship called a trireme. Triremes were designed to ram enemy ships and hole them below the waterline. A ram was usually made of bronze. The ships fought battles by breaking through lines of enemy boats, turning, ramming, and then moving out of reach.

## A SPARTAN WAY OF LIFE

The city state of Sparta controlled the southern part of Greece, called the Peloponnese. After the Spartans conquered Messenia, they became obsessed with holding onto power. To quell rebellions and repel foreign invasions, they dedicated themselves to war. All true Spartans had to be warriors; the training, which started at the age of seven, was extremely tough. Boys were often whipped to prepare them for the pain and fear of the battlefield. Girls also trained to be fit and strong, so they would give birth to healthy Spartan babies. Their military skill helped Sparta to win the Peloponnesian Wars fought against Athens during 431-404 BC.

This bronze figure shows a tough Spartan warrior in all his glory. Spartan soldiers wore helmets, breastplates, and leg coverings called greaves to protect themselves.

*At harvest time, women separated the grain from the chaff.*

**Byzantium**

**THRACE**

*In 480 BC, the Persians marched their army into Greece.*

**Troy**

**LEMNOS**

*One of the most famous Greek poets was a woman named Sappho from the island of Lesbos.*

**LESBOS**

*Women wore dresses in the Ionic (left) or Doric (right) styles.*

**CHIOS**

**Ephesus**

**SAMOS**

**Miletus**

*Herodotus was the first person to try to record events accurately. He is called the "father of history."*

**NAXOS**

**Halicarnassus**

**THERA**

*Shortage of food on Thera forced some islanders to leave and try to set up a colony in north Africa. But when they gave up and tried to come home, the people would not let them land.*

**RHODES**

*Greek warships were called triremes. They had three levels of oarsmen on each side.*

## THE CITY OF ATHENS

Athens became the largest and most prosperous city state in Greece. It controlled the silver mines in the south and had excellent trading links from its port at Piraeus. Standing above the main city of Athens was the rocky hill called the Acropolis, which means "high city." It was a sacred place with beautiful temples and shrines to the goddess Athene. The rest of the city was built at the foot of the hill. Athens had splendid buildings, paved streets, and an open market and general meeting place called the *agora*. Scholars like Socrates, Plato, and Aristotle taught there.

**The Acropolis in Athens**

*The temple called the Erechtheum contained a very ancient wooden statue of Athene.*

*The great altar stood at the side of Athene's temple, instead of in front, as was usual.*

*The main temple of the goddess Athene was called the Parthenon. It was built from brilliant white marble in 447-438 BC. The roof was made of marble tiles.*

*A colored frieze showed the battle of the centaurs, mythical Greek figures who were half-man, half-horse.*

*A huge bronze statue of the goddess Athene the Defender stood 30 ft (9 m) tall.*

*Great religious processions wound their way through Athens. They entered the sacred enclosure on the Acropolis through a gateway called the Propylaea.*

*The temple of Athene Nike, the goddess in her role as bringer of victory.*

**MEDITERRANEAN SEA**

| 0 | 25 | 50 | 75 | 100 Kilometers |

| 0 | 25 | 50 | 75 Miles |

# GREECE – ALEXANDER AND AFTER

ALEXANDER THE GREAT was one of the finest generals the world had ever known. He was a brave soldier whose campaigns were brilliantly planned. By 323 BC, he had conquered an empire that stretched from Greece to Asia Minor and all the way to India. Alexander's career of conquest took him on a military journey that lasted 11 years, covering more than 20,000 miles (32,000 km).

Alexander was born in 356 BC in the kingdom of Macedonia, once an enemy of Athens. After the murder of his father, King Philip II, the 20-year-old Alexander

became king. He inherited a large and experienced army of Greeks and Macedonians and completed his father's plan to finish off the hated Persians.

During his long campaign, Alexander left men behind in all the lands he conquered. This helped spread the Greek language and culture over an enormous area. Some of the world's most impressive building styles were established and important ideas were absorbed into later civilizations. Although Alexander achieved a godlike status, he died of a fever while preparing to invade Arabia.

### ALEXANDER THE GREAT

Alexander traveled huge distances to extend the borders of his empire. Along the route of his conquests, he founded cities, all named Alexandria. The most famous and long-lived is the one in Egypt. He had little time to run his vast empire but tried to get Greeks and his new subjects to be friendly with each other. But when Alexander died, his generals murdered Alexander's wife, Roxane, and his young son, who would have posed a threat. Then they fought each other for control of the empire. Antigonus took Greece, Ptolemy got Egypt, and Seleucus held the Middle East.

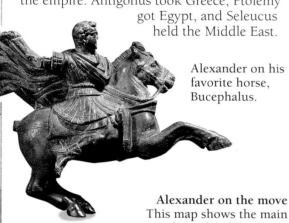

Alexander on his favorite horse, Bucephalus.

#### Alexander on the move
This map shows the main events in Alexander's life. While taking the kingdoms of Asia Minor, Alexander won two great battles against the Persians at Granicus and Issus. He turned south, taking Phoenicia, Judea, and Egypt, where he was accepted as pharaoh. He then beat the Persians at Gaugamela, before going to India, where he was victorious at the Hydaspes River. He would have gone on, but his troops were exhausted.

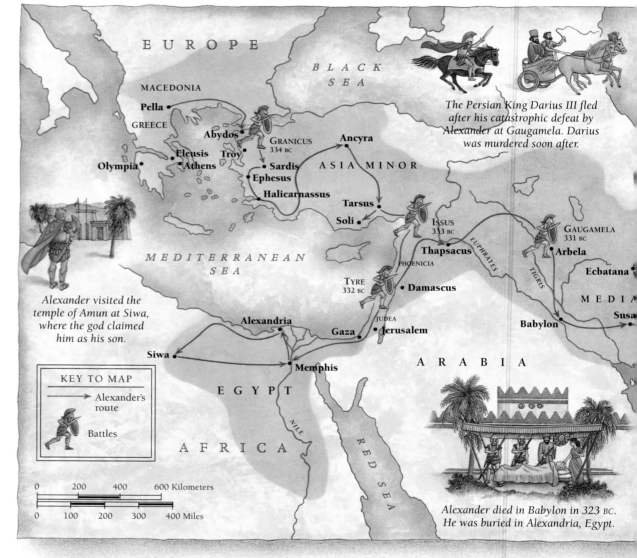

The Persian King Darius III fled after his catastrophic defeat by Alexander at Gaugamela. Darius was murdered soon after.

Alexander visited the temple of Amun at Siwa, where the god claimed him as his son.

**KEY TO MAP**
→ Alexander's route
Battles

0  200  400  600 Kilometers
0  100  200  300  400 Miles

Alexander died in Babylon in 323 BC. He was buried in Alexandria, Egypt.

### GODS AND GODDESSES

The Greeks had 12 major deities – five of them are shown on the right. The others were Hera, goddess of women and wife of Zeus, and her sister Hestia, guardian of the hearth and home. There was Apollo, god of the Sun and music and twin brother of Artemis. Aphrodite was goddess of love and beauty, while Pluto was god of the Underworld. Ares (son of Zeus and Hera) was god of war. Hermes, son of one of one of the many loves of Zeus, was the messenger of the gods. There were other, less important, gods who cared for different aspects of life and death.

Artemis, the huntress, was goddess of the Moon, protector of women and children.

Zeus was king of the gods. He controlled the thunder. The eagle was his special bird.

Demeter was goddess of the grain. She had the power to make wheat, barley, and all living things grow.

Poseidon was god of the sea. He was also brother of Zeus and Pluto. He holds a trident, symbol of the fisherman.

Athene, daughter of Zeus, was the goddess of wisdom and war and the patroness of Athens. The owl was the symbol of Athene.

## A THIRST FOR KNOWLEDGE

In the 6th century BC, Greek scholars began trying to find out all they could about life and the Universe and how it worked. Such men were called philosophers, meaning "lovers of knowledge." They asked questions about how the body worked, calculated mathematical problems, and watched the movement of the planets. Alexander's tutor Aristotle described and studied several hundred species of animal. These early Greek studies formed the basis of modern biology, medicine, mathematics, astronomy, and philosophy.

Pythagoras was born on the Greek island of Samos in about 560 BC. He was an astronomer and mathematician, who is remembered for his work with triangles.

*A series of columns surrounded the temple. A main room housed the statue of a god or goddess, and a storeroom held the temple treasure.*

*The exterior was decorated with reliefs and statues, painted mainly in the traditional colors red and blue.*

The Greeks built impressive temples for their gods. The remains of this Doric temple, dedicated to Poseidon, stand in southern Italy.

*A Greek temple was built on a stepped platform.*

## BUILT TO LAST

Most homes in Greece were fairly simple buildings made of brick and wood with earth floors. The Greeks lavished all their money and skill on public buildings, especially their temples. Although they were originally made of wood and thatch, from the 6th century BC onward, temples were made of stone or marble, with roofs of baked clay tiles. The architects took care to achieve a look of balance and harmony. Many Greek buildings were decorated with vertical pillars, or columns. There were two main styles – Doric, which was a simple style with sturdy, plain columns; and Ionic, which was more elegant, with thinner, decorated columns. Many public buildings were also adorned with friezes and statues, and some had wall paintings.

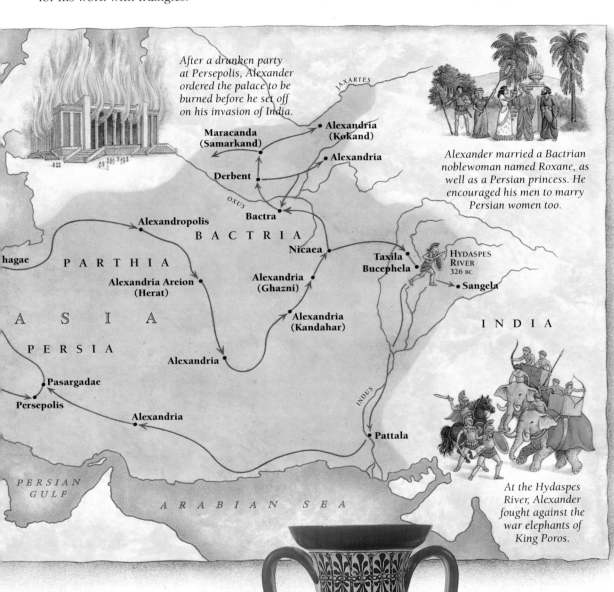

*After a drunken party at Persepolis, Alexander ordered the palace to be burned before he set off on his invasion of India.*

*Alexander married a Bactrian noblewoman named Roxane, as well as a Persian princess. He encouraged his men to marry Persian women too.*

*At the Hydaspes River, Alexander fought against the war elephants of King Poros.*

JAXARTES

Maracanda (Samarkand)

Alexandria (Køkand)

Alexandria

Derbent

OXUS

Alexandropolis

Bactra

BACTRIA

Nicaea

Taxila
Bucephela

HYDASPES RIVER 326 BC

hagae

PARTHIA

Alexandria Areion (Herat)

Alexandria (Ghazni)

Sangela

A S I A

PERSIA

Alexandria (Kandahar)

I N D I A

Alexandria

Pasargadae

Persepolis

Alexandria

INDUS

Pattala

PERSIAN GULF

A R A B I A N   S E A

This is the Greek theater at Miletus in modern Turkey. It is still used for plays.

## THE OLYMPIC GAMES

Athletics contests were held as part of all important religious festivals in Greece. The most important were the Olympic Games, which were held every four years and lasted five days. As it was the duty of every male citizen to fight for his city state in wartime, he had to keep himself physically fit. Many of the events at the games, such as throwing the javelin, wrestling, or boxing, were based on military skills. During the games, all wars had to stop, so contestants could travel in safety to Olympia from all over the Greek world. The winners often became famous stars.

Greek red and black figure ware was made from clay found around Athens. This vase is decorated with figures in a chariot race. This was one of the events in the Olympic Games. Other events included running, the pentathlon, discus throwing, and horse racing. Women were not allowed to take part in, or even to watch, the games.

## DRAMA

The first great plays were written by the Greeks. As part of the Dionysia, a festival in Athens to honor the god Dionysus, poets composed and performed songs. These gradually got longer, with more and more performers taking part, until the songs had grown into plays. There were three types of plays – comedies, tragedies, and satires, which poked fun at serious topics. Prizes were awarded for the best new play in each category. Special open-air theaters were built in which to perform plays. Only men were allowed to perform, and all the actors wore masks.

# ROME – FROM VILLAGES TO EMPIRE

THE ROMAN EMPIRE was the largest and most powerful force the western world had ever seen. By AD 220, under the rule of the emperors, Rome controlled most of Europe, North Africa, and a large part of the Middle East. But the story of the Romans began about 750 BC, with a group of farmers who lived on the hills overlooking the Tiber River. Gradually, their villages merged into one powerful city. Before long, the tough peasants, who made excellent soldiers, began to dominate the people around them. By 264 BC, they had taken over the whole of Italy.

Over the years, the Romans became even more ambitious. They trained huge armies to conquer and control their territories and built a network of roads to move their armies around. They introduced their Latin language, their distinctive style of building, and their system of government to the conquered areas. When the western part of the empire collapsed in AD 476, many things were left behind that still influence our way of life today.

This bust shows Octavian, the first emperor of Rome. In 27 BC, he was given the title of Augustus, which means "the revered one."

## RULERS OF ROME

At first, Rome was ruled by kings. Then, in about 507 BC, the Romans set up a republic – a government run by the nobles who were elected by the citizens. This lasted nearly 500 years. But by 49 BC, Rome was plunged into a bloody civil war. To restore peace, the Romans gave power to one man – Octavian – who became the first Roman emperor. Some later emperors, such as Trajan, were popular and ruled well, but others were cruel. Domitian murdered anyone who disagreed with him, and Caligula was so crazy that he made his horse a senator.

Julius Caesar was a famous Roman general. He was assassinated by rival politicians on March 15, 44 BC.

*Ships stayed in port from November to March to avoid winter storms.*

Roman engineers built this impressive aqueduct in Segovia to carry water to the city from the surrounding hills.

*In about AD 122, the Emperor Hadrian ordered the building of a massive stone wall to defend the northern frontier.*

BRITAIN

**Londinium** (London)

SILCHESTER

*Julius Caesar conquered Gaul (58-51 BC), and twice invaded Britain in 55-54 BC.*

GAUL

*Hannibal, a Carthaginian general, attacked Rome in 218 BC. He marched 40,000 men and 37 elephants across the Alps.*

**Burdigala** (Bordeaux)

NIMES

**Massilia** (Marseilles)

**Tarraco** (Tarragona)

*Supplies of grain and olive oil were shipped to the port of Ostia, just south of Rome.*

ATLANTIC OCEAN

HISPANIA

ITALICA

**Gades** (Cadiz)

**Carthago Nova** (Cartagena)

MEDI

ROMAN ROAD

AFRICA

## THE SENATE

During the Republic, Rome was governed by two officials, called consuls. They were assisted by the Senate, a group of men (senators) who passed the laws. At first, all the senators came from the rich (patrician) families of Rome. Both the consuls and government officials were voted into office each year by the ordinary citizens (plebeians). Later, after strikes and demonstrations, the plebeians were given the power to stop laws from being passed. However, the emperors took this power away.

*A senator wore a white robe, or toga, with a purple stripe around the edge.*

300 BC
100 BC
AD 220

BRITAIN
GERMANY
GAUL
HISPANIA
Rome
ITALY
ANATOLIA
MEDITERRANEAN SEA
SYRIA
AFRICA
EGYPT

This map shows how the Roman empire grew from about 300 BC to about AD 220, when it reached its greatest extent.

0  100  200  300  400 Kilometers
0  100  200  300 Miles

## ROAD BUILDERS

The Romans built a huge network of roads across their empire. These roads helped the army move quickly into battle, provided a route for a postal system, and made trade easier. The roads ran straight, using bridges or viaducts – a series of arches – to cross any rivers or steep-sided valleys. Roman roads were so well built that they survived for hundreds of years after the empire had ended. Many European roads still follow the direct route taken by the Roman roads.

**A permanent camp for the Roman army**

*Stables for the horses*

*Headquarters building*

*The barracks were crowded, with up to 80 soldiers in each block.*

*Soldiers built a high wall with watchtowers to defend the camp.*

*Border patrols spent their time quelling local uprisings.*

**Augusta Treverorum (Trier)**

*The Emperor Marcus Aurelius defended his empire against invasion on the frontier along the Danube River.*

### THE ROMAN ARMY

The Romans were able to conquer and rule their huge empire because of their army. They had the best-trained, best-equipped army in the world. Roman armies, divided into groups called legions, fought in formation using swords and spears and protecting themselves with shields. Each night, they built a temporary camp and then dismantled it in the morning. On the frontiers of the empire, there were permanent forts for the troops.

*Every legion had its own standard, carried by the standard bearer. The silver eagle was the symbol of Jupiter, king of the Roman gods.*

### BIGGER AND BETTER BUILDINGS

At first, the Romans copied many of the Greek building styles. But in the 2nd century BC, they discovered how to make concrete out of volcanic ash. This allowed them to build much bigger and stronger structures. They developed the arch, which took the weight of a building and let them span greater distances than was possible before. They used the arch to build bridges, aqueducts, and amphitheaters, like the Colosseum in Rome, where people watched gladiator fights.

*At the heart of every Roman city was an open space called the forum. Some of the buildings of the forum in Rome are still standing.*

### RELIGION

The Romans worshiped many gods and goddesses who looked after various aspects of their life. Venus, for example, was the goddess of love and beauty, and Mars was the god of war. Then a new religion – Christianity – became popular. Its followers believed that Jesus Christ was the son of the one God of the Jews. Although Jesus was put to death, Christianity spread rapidly, and in 391 AD it became the official faith of the empire.

**GERMANY**

*RHINE*

**CARNUNTUM**

*DANUBE*

**ALPS**

**Aquileia**

*Barbarians, the Roman name for foreign invaders, finally overran the Roman Empire. The most famous group was led by Attila the Hun.*

**Viminacium**

*DANUBE*

*ROMAN ROAD*

**Durostorum (Silistra)**

**B L A C K   S E A**

*TIBER*

**CORSICA**

**Rome**

**THE ROMAN COLOSSEUM**

*ADRIATIC SEA*

**ITALY**

**SARDINIA**

*Marble was quarried in Greece for the fine buildings in Rome.*

**Byzantium (Istanbul)**

**Trapezus (Trabzon)**

**A N A T O L I A**

*Wild animals were brought from India and Africa to fight in arenas across the empire.*

*ROMAN ROAD*

*IONIAN SEA*

**GREECE**

*AEGEAN SEA*

**Ephesus**

*TRADE ROUTE FROM CHINA*

**Rhegium (Reggio di Calabria)**

**SICILY**

**Syracuse**

**Carthage**

**Antioch**

**CYPRUS**

**S Y R I A**

*M E D I T E R R A N E A N   S E A*

**EL DJEM**

**CRETE**

*Trade ship takes grain and linen from Egypt to Rome.*

*Rome and Carthage battled at sea for control of Sicily during the first Punic War (264-241 BC).*

**Leptis Magna**

*The road was raised in the center so rainwater ran into the ditches at the sides.*

*The road was paved with thick slabs of hardwearing stone.*

*Workers, often slaves, dug a trench, which they filled with layers of stones and gravel.*

*Cleopatra of Egypt married Mark Antony, a Roman general. They killed themselves after defeat by Octavian at the Battle of Actium (31 BC).*

**Alexandria**

**Jerusalem**

**JUDEA**

*Jesus Christ was crucified in the Roman province of Judea during the reign of the Emperor Tiberius.*

*TRADE ROUTE FROM INDIA*

*NILE*

**E G Y P T**

*RED SEA*

39

# ROME – LIFE IN THE CITY

ABOUT ONE MILLION PEOPLE were crowded into the city of Rome by AD 300. It was a magnificent city, with palaces for the emperor and his family and beautiful houses for the very rich. Throughout the city, emperors set up statues of themselves; triumphal arches and columns celebrated their victories. There were several forums – open spaces used as markets and for social and political gatherings – as well as theaters, libraries, public baths, and shops selling goods from all over the empire. Life for the rich was very pleasant.

The poor people did not do so well. They lived in overcrowded apartment blocks in areas that were dirty, noisy, smelly, and often downright dangerous. The buildings were badly built with so many floors that they often collapsed or caught fire, killing the people inside. Life was even worse for the thousands of slaves who were brought back to Rome as the empire grew. They had to do all the dirty, heavy work or train to fight – and probably die – as gladiators in the Colosseum.

*The official garment of a Roman citizen was the toga. It was made from a large piece of semicircular white woollen cloth, worn over a tunic.*

*The tunic was usually worn on its own by poorer people, who found it more comfortable for work.*

*A woman wore a fine wool tunic. Over this came a stola, a dress that reached to her feet. A garment called a palla could be draped over the stola.*

The Romans loved an excuse to celebrate. This procession shows the festival of Ceriales, held every April to honor Ceres, the goddess of corn. It was painted by Sir Lawrence Alma-Tadema (1836-1912).

### FAMILY LIFE

The father was the head of his family, which included his grandchildren and slaves. He even held the power of life and death over them. A new baby had to be accepted into the family by its father, or it would be left outside to die. Once accepted, a baby was a good reason for a party, and the house was decorated with leaves and flower garlands. After nine days of life, a baby boy was given a protective charm called a *bulla*, to wear around his neck. When children grew older, their parents decided whom they would marry.

*Girls and boys wore tunics. When a boy was 14, he went to the forum with his family. There he took off his childhood charm and put on the toga of an adult male citizen.*

### GOING TO SCHOOL

Rich parents sent their sons to school or educated them at home with private tutors, who were often Greek. Boys went to school when they were about six. They learned basic reading, writing, and mathematics. When they were 11, they went to a more advanced teacher, the *grammaticus*, and they studied literature, history, math, and astronomy. By the age of 14, those who wanted to be politicians went on to study rhetoric (public speaking). Girls learned household skills at home. Poorer children never had a chance – they had to go to work.

**A scene inside a Roman house**

*Tiles were made from a clay mold, then baked until hard.*

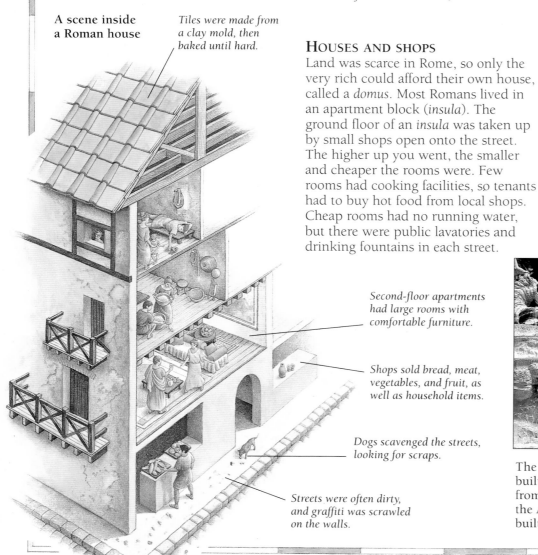

### HOUSES AND SHOPS

Land was scarce in Rome, so only the very rich could afford their own house, called a *domus*. Most Romans lived in an apartment block (*insula*). The ground floor of an *insula* was taken up by small shops open onto the street. The higher up you went, the smaller and cheaper the rooms were. Few rooms had cooking facilities, so tenants had to buy hot food from local shops. Cheap rooms had no running water, but there were public lavatories and drinking fountains in each street.

*Second-floor apartments had large rooms with comfortable furniture.*

*Shops sold bread, meat, vegetables, and fruit, as well as household items.*

*Dogs scavenged the streets, looking for scraps.*

*Streets were often dirty, and graffiti was scrawled on the walls.*

The Trevi Fountain (above) was built around AD 1750 to use water from the ancient Roman aqueduct, the Aqua Virgo. The aqueduct was built during the reign of Augustus.

### WATER WORKS

Rome needed huge amounts of water each day to supply the public baths, lavatories, and drinking fountains. The water was brought into the city by aqueduct, a large bridge with a channel to carry water. Rich people had water piped directly to their homes, but they had to pay for it according to the size of the lead pipes they used. Many people tried to avoid paying, by secretly joining their pipes into the main network. The public baths were huge buildings with hot and cold pools, where thousands of people went for a bath or a massage or just to gossip.

CITY WALL

## Map of Rome

This map shows the layout of Rome in about AD 300. Temples, triumphal arches, forums, bath houses, grand tombs called mausoleums, and aqueducts were set up by different emperors and named after them. The wall to defend the city was built by the Emperor Aurelian in AD 270.

| KEY TO MAP | |
|---|---|
| 1 Mausoleum of Hadrian | 8 Camp of the Praetorian Guard |
| 2 Mausoleum of Augustus | 9 Forum of Trajan |
| 3 Gardens of Lucullus | 10 Roman Forum |
| 4 Arch of Claudius | 11 Tiber Island |
| 5 Stadium of Domitian | 12 Colosseum |
| 6 Pantheon of Hadrian | 13 Trajan Baths |
| 7 Baths of Diocletian | 14 Temple of Claudius |
| | 15 Circus Maximus |
| | 16 Baths of Caracalla |

This mosaic shows gladiators trying to kill each other. Gladiators were criminals or slaves trained to fight for the entertainment of the people.

### HOME DECORATING

The Romans admired Greek art and used Greek sculptors and artists to decorate their buildings and homes. City houses were often plain on the outside. The rich Romans painted the inside walls with scenes from mythology or with gardens or the countryside. Elegant statues of gods and goddesses were also placed around the house. Floors were covered with mosaics – pictures and patterns made from small pieces of colored stone. A wealthy home would also have elegant furniture of wood, bronze, and marble, and perhaps a display of antique Greek vases.

This painting shows what a battlefield the Colosseum could be. The Romans adored the idea of exotic animals. Lions, tigers, leopards, rhinoceroses, and bears were brought from all over the world, to fight for the crowds.

### THE ROMAN GAMES

The Romans loved to be entertained. The most popular events were chariot races, gladiator fights, or wild beast hunts. The games attracted huge crowds, who placed money on who would win the races or the fights. The bloodthirsty crowds watched wild beasts fight each other, often to the death. Gladiators also fought each other using swords, nets, and spears in their struggle to survive. Gladiators were named after the sword, or *gladius*, that they carried. If a gladiator was wounded, the crowd decided whether he would live or die by giving the "thumbs-up" or "thumbs-down" sign.

Every five years, Romans were registered in a *census*, a head count to see how many citizens there were and who might be available to fight. Anyone who was a citizen in Rome was entitled to claim the dole (a free handout) of grain. The *census*, shown left, took place during a religious festival in which a bull, sheep, and pig were sacrificed.

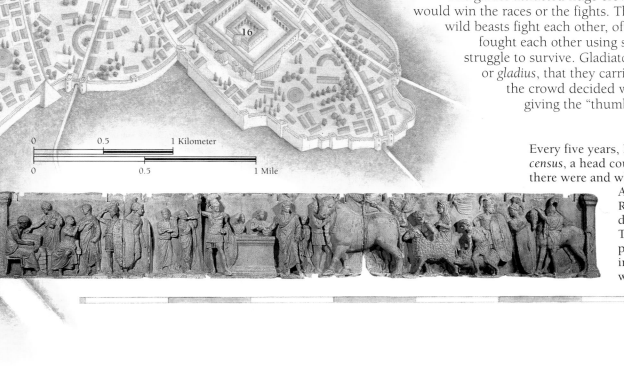

# THE RICHES OF ARABIA

THE DESERTS OF ARABIA are among the hottest and driest places in the world. The people who lived in these hostile lands belonged to nomadic tribes that moved with their animals from one water hole to another, feeding on the vegetation that grew briefly after the light winter rains. Along the fertile coasts of the west and south, however, there were busy trading cities with paved roads and settled peoples. In the city of Mecca, one of the world's great religions, Islam, was born.

In the southern kingdoms, the Arabs enjoyed fabulous riches. They built a spectacular dam at Ma'rib, which controlled the water supply for their agriculture. But it was trade that made the Arabs rich. Resin from frankincense and myrrh trees provided neighboring civilizations with incense for their religious ceremonies. Merchants traded in gold, gems, and ivory, as well as copper, tin, and iron, and wide-ranging trade networks reached not only the Mediterranean world but also East Africa, India, and China.

Palmyra

TRADE ROUTE TO ROME

Tyre

MEDITERRANEAN SEA

Alexandria

NABATAEA

Petra

SINAI

*Nabataean craftsmen made finely decorated pots.*

Taym

E G Y P T

Berenice

R E D

## LIFE IN THE DESERT

The name given to the nomadic Arab was *bedouin*, meaning "desert dweller." Each family lived in a large goats' hair tent with a few personal belongings. These tents provided shade from the sun, and they were warm in the cold desert nights. The *bedouin* grazed sheep and goats and later raised horses and camels. The camel made an enormous difference when it was tamed in about 1100 BC. Camels can travel up to 100 miles (160 km) a day for eight days without water in extreme heat. People could now cross the deserts, which they had not been able to do before.

Arabs used camels very effectively in battle. This stone carving from Assyria shows how Arab rulers fought off Assyrian invasions.

Temples, tombs, and monuments were cut out of the bare rock face in the city of Petra in modern-day Jordan. This building, probably built in about 100 BC, was the *khasneh*, or treasury. Petra is situated in a valley surrounded by cliffs. It has only one very narrow entrance, which made it easy to defend.

## THE NABATAEANS

The Nabataeans were an Arab tribe that lived in the northern part of Arabia. In the 4th century BC they founded a kingdom that covered the earlier biblical land of Edom. Their capital city was Petra, which controlled the overland route for incense from southern Arabia. They also had the only reliable source of water in the area, which they brought into the city through a series of channels and earthenware pipes. At the height of their power, in the 1st century AD, the Nabataeans controlled the areas as far north as Damascus, but the Romans took over their kingdom in 106 AD.

## LIFE OF MOHAMMED — AD 571-632

The Prophet Mohammed was a camel caravan leader who became deeply interested in religion. After years of prayer and thought, he believed he received a revelation from the One God, Allah. It was his mission to preach a new faith which involved submitting to the will of God. At first his message was not well received by the people of his home town of Mecca. He fled to Medina but returned in AD 630 with a victorious army. After this, the new faith, Islam, spread rapidly. Its members are called Muslims.

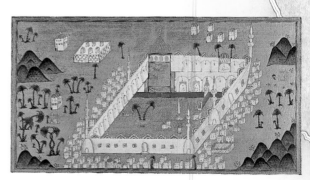

This tile painting shows the Holy Mosque of the Prophet Mohammed in Medina. The mosque houses the tomb of Mohammed, making Medina one of Islam's holiest cities.

Muslim pilgrims in Mecca pray before the Kaaba, the shrine under the black veil. The Kaaba is said to have been built by Abraham.

## FROM MANY GODS TO ONE

The early Arabs worshiped several deities, including the Moon god and his wife the goddess of the Sun, as well as Atarsamain, goddess of love, whose symbol was the morning star. But the Prophet Mohammed preached that there was only One God, Allah. Muslims have five religious duties. They must believe in the One God and acknowledge that Mohammed is his Prophet. They pray five times a day, facing Mecca. They should also give alms to the poor, fast during the month they call Ramadan, and visit Mecca at least once in their lives.

TRADE ROUTE TO CHINA

The map on the right shows the growth of the Islamic Empire between AD 632, when Mohammed died, and AD 750, when the expansion ended.

EUROPE

BLACK SEA

CASPIAN SEA

JAXARTES

OXUS

ASIA

Cordoba
Granada
Fez
MEDITERRANEAN SEA
Alexandria
Cairo
Damascus
Jerusalem
EUPHRATES
Baghdad
Isfahan
Kabul
INDUS

AFRICA

NILE

Medina
ARABIA
Mecca

INDIA

ARABIAN SEA

AD 632

AD 750

### THE SPREAD OF ISLAM

Inspired by their new faith of Islam, the Arabs surged out of Arabia. Through war and conquest, they rapidly captured a vast empire that stretched across the Middle East to India and across North Africa into southern Europe. As they went, they converted the majority of the inhabitants to Islam. They also absorbed much from the culture and learning of their new provinces, creating a glorious new civilization of their own.

MESOPOTAMIA

EUPHRATES

*Queen Zenobia ruled the great trading city of Palmyra and united many Arab provinces against their Roman masters. She was eventually captured by the Emperor Aurelian and taken to Rome.*

*Arab chiefs used saluki dogs to hunt. Lions were the greatest prize, but they are now extinct in the area.*

NEFUD DESERT

PERSIAN GULF

PERSIA

*Bedouin lived in tents made from woven goats' hair. Although camels were essential to their survival, horses were their great passion.*

DILMUN (BAHRAIN)

*Arab ships called dhows traded with India and Africa.*

TRADE ROUTE TO INDIA

**Medina**

*Thousands of warriors rode into the defeated city of Mecca on the first pilgrimage.*

*Merchants traveled overland by camel in groups called caravans.*

**Mecca**

A R A B I A

RUB' AL KHALI DESERT

*Only Muslims may enter the city of Mecca, the most holy city of Islam.*

*When the bark of frankincense and myrrh trees was cut, the resin was collected and used as incense.*

S E A

*The dam at Ma'rib was built in the 7th century BC. It broke in the 6th century AD, causing terrible damage.*

**Shibam**

HADHRAMAUT

These terraced fields in the southwest corner of Arabia, in modern-day Yemen, show the crops after the August rain.

### FORTUNATE ARABIA

Along the fertile coasts of Arabia there was enough water to grow grain, fruits, and vegetables. The Romans, who knew only of the fertile areas and the wealth gained from the incense trade, showed an interest in Arabia. They called the country "Fortunate Arabia." The Emperor Augustus sent an expedition into the interior in 25 BC, but when they found a land of scorching sand, all ideas of conquest were abandoned.

SABAEA

**Ma'rib**

AXUM

*Harvesting apricots*

**Qana**

QATABAN

*There is archaeological evidence to suggest that multistory houses of mud brick existed in the 3rd and 4th centuries BC.*

**Aden**

*The people of Axum, who were descended from southern Arabs, invaded in AD 570 and marched toward Mecca. A smallpox epidemic is said to have forced them to withdraw.*

TRADE ROUTE TO INDIA

GULF OF ADEN

0    100    200    300 Kilometers

0    50    100    150    200 Miles

# AFRICA – KINGDOMS OF GOLD

AFRICA IS A VAST CONTINENT where the first humans are thought to have evolved. From about AD 700, fabulous kingdoms rose and fell, isolated from the rest of the world by the huge wastes of the Sahara Desert. More than 3,000 years ago, Africa south of the Sahara was inhabited by tribal peoples who lived by hunting and gathering. Gradually, however, Bantu-speaking people migrated out of the forests of West Africa and made their way east and south. They reached the area around the Congo River by about 500 BC and southern Africa by about AD 400.

Some of the first great African cities emerged in the Bantu heartland of West Africa. Kingdoms such as Ghana, Mali, Songhay, and Benin traded gold with the Muslims who had invaded North Africa in the 8th century AD. Over to the east was Meroë, Africa's first great civilization outside of Egypt. To the south, the impressive stone fortress kingdom of Great Zimbabwe was built. The city was a major religious, political, and trading center for southern Africa.

This gold papyrus holder belonged to King Aspelta of Cush. It was found near Napata and dates from about 590 BC.

## KINGDOM OF MEROE

To the south of Egypt lay the lands of Nubia and Cush. For a time the peoples of these regions were dominated by Egypt. Then, in 728 BC, they seized power over Egypt and ruled it for almost 100 years. Finally they withdrew south and, in the 3rd century BC, set up their capital at Meroë. They built an impressive royal residence of brick and stone, a temple for their lion god Apedemak, and steep-sided pyramid tombs. Their art, architecture, and religion were influenced by Egypt, but evolved into a unique style. The Meroites were also among the earliest people to develop an alphabet. They raised cattle, grew cotton, and used waterwheels driven by oxen to water their fields. The population included skilled ironworkers and prosperous merchants who traded with the Mediterranean world and India. Meroë was finally overrun in the 4th century AD by people from Axum.

*The Phoenician colony of Carthage dominated trade until it was destroyed by the Romans in 146 BC.*

*Ibn Battuta was born in Tangier and became a great traveler. On one journey (AD 1352–1353) he crossed the Sahara and reached as far south as the Niger River.*

*Jenne was an important trading center. Its mosque, made of mud and wood, dominated the city.*

*Gold was mined in the forests of West Africa.*

*One of the terra-cotta heads made by the Nok people. The Nok culture flourished from about 500 BC to AD 200.*

*The domesticated camel came into use in the Sahara in about 100 BC. Merchants regularly made the difficult journey across the desert.*

*Arab conquerors built Cairo, which became one of the most important cities of the Muslim world.*

*Queen Mothers in Meroë, such as Amanirenas and Amanishakheto, held positions of great power. Here one is presented with an ox.*

*In the 13th century AD, under the direction of King Lalibela, 10 Christian churches were cut out of rock. Pilgrims trekked vast distances to visit them.*

TRADE ROUTE TO INDIA AND CHINA

ARABIA

RED SEA

MEDITERRANEAN SEA

Tangier

Fez

Marrakesh

Carthage

Leptis Magna

Alexandria

Cairo

EGYPT

NUBIA

CUSH

Napata

MEROE

Meroë

Axum

AXUM

Lalibela

Mogadishu

NILE

WHITE NILE

BLUE NILE

SAHARA DESERT

KANEM

LAKE CHAD

BORNO

Timbuktu

Gao

Taghaza

Jenne

SONGHAY

MALI

GHANA

NIGER

Nok

Ife

BENIN

Igbo Ukwu

AKAN

AFRICA

## BANTU-SPEAKING PEOPLE

The Bantu speakers were herders and farmers who spread across the continent from West Africa. Their superior knowledge of ironworking enabled them to make tools and weapons. This helped their migration to other parts of Africa. Techniques of smelting iron were often passed from father to son, and smiths held a special status in the community. The Bantu found a route into the Congo basin, and another that went east and then south. As they advanced, the hunter-gatherers who had lived there before them retreated into places the Bantu did not want.

## GREAT KINGDOMS

West Africa saw the rise and fall of several great kingdoms – Ghana (AD 700-1200), Mali (AD 1200-1500), and Songhay (AD 1350-1600). Gold was the main source of their wealth. Merchants brought goods from the Mediterranean to the cities on the southern fringes of the Sahara and exchanged them for gold, as well as slaves, sandalwood, hides, and kola nuts. Meanwhile, the imported goods were shipped to the West African kingdoms and into the interior. Many people in African kingdoms were converted to Islam through contact with Muslim traders.

This terracotta figure from the 12th century AD was excavated from a burial mound near Jenne.

This bronze head shows a Queen Mother of Benin. Spectacular heads and figures were made by the people of Benin from the 14th century AD.

## FOREST KINGDOM OF BENIN

The kingdom of Benin was founded in the 11th century AD in the forests of what is now Nigeria. It was known to its own people as Edo. The kingdom rose to power during the 14th century AD, when it was ruled by Ewuare the Great, who was known as the *oba*, or ruler. The *oba* lived in an enormous palace in the walled city of Benin. Merchants traded ivory, pepper, palm oil, and slaves with the Portuguese. The Edo people had no written language, so records of their history were passed on by word of mouth. On special occasions, an official recited Benin's history from memory.

TRADE ROUTE TO INDIA AND CHINA

### MADAGASCAR

Women in Madagascar used wooden hoes to prepare the ground for sowing millet, a crop introduced from the mainland.

Great ports grew up along the east coast where local rulers traded with Arab merchants. This merchant is weighing gold dust.

LAKE VICTORIA

Zanzibar

Malindi
Mombasa

Kilwa

LAKE TANGANYIKA

LAKE NYASA

ZAMBEZI

Great Zimbabwe

Sofala

Along Africa's great rivers, many villages depended on fishing for their livelihood.

The Bantu-speakers were great ironworkers. They used clay kilns which were fueled with wood charcoal.

From about AD 1270-1450 the stone-walled city of Great Zimbabwe was the capital of a large Shona Empire.

KALAHARI DESERT

ORANGE

A woman collects pods from an acacia tree on the fringes of the Kalahari Desert.

The lives of the Khoikhoi, who migrated into southern Africa, revolved around their cattle.

I N D I A N   O C E A N

0  250  500  750  1000 Kilometers
0  250  500  750 Miles

A T L A N T I C   O C E A N

This ivory horn was carved by African craftworkers in the 16th century AD. It was made for export and bears the Portuguese coat of arms.

## TRADING KINGDOMS OF EAST AFRICA

Gold and ivory, slaves, copper and iron, emeralds, spices, and animal skins drew merchants to the east coast of Africa from the Muslim world and from as far afield as India and China. The rulers of the coastal cities, such as Mogadishu, Malindi, and Kilwa, acted as middlemen. All goods from the interior had to pass through their cities, where they were able to charge tax on them. This trade made the east coast ports and their rulers very rich indeed. The Sultan of Kilwa, for example, had a magnificent palace with more than 100 rooms and a beautiful bathing pool.

## AXUM

The kingdom of Axum lay near the southern end of the Red Sea. It was in a good position for trading ivory, incense, and spices. The Axumites became rich and powerful in the 3rd century AD under King Ezana (AD 320-350). During the 6th century AD the Axumites conquered part of Arabia and ruled it for a time. Most of the population were craftworkers, builders, or farmers. Axum was one of the first African states to adopt Christianity.

Towers up to 100 ft (30 m) tall were carved with scenes showing different aspects of religion.

**The City of Axum**

The royal palace of Takija Mariam was the most important building in the city.

Blocks of limestone and marble were used to build the palaces and other important buildings.

Most people lived in round homes made of mud and thatch.

# INDIA – THE MAURYAN AGE

A DYNASTY OF KINGS called the Mauryans ruled India from 322-185 BC. They came to power hundreds of years after the collapse of the great Indus Valley civilization. By about 600 BC, the Aryan invaders of the Indus Valley had merged with the rest of the Indian population. They introduced their Sanskrit language and composed their sacred hymns, called the *Vedas*, that laid the foundation of society and their Hindu religion. But the country was still divided into small rival kingdoms that were constantly challenging each other for overall power.

However, there was a bigger threat from the west. In 330 BC, Alexander the Great, who had recently defeated the Persians, marched his army into India. But the troops were exhausted and, after a few months, they headed home. It was at this point that a young Indian warrior, Chandragupta Maurya, seized power. First he overthrew the ruling kingdom of Magadha. Then he challenged the Greek general Seleucus, who had taken over part of Alexander's empire. Chandragupta proved to be a clever ruler and a great soldier. By the time his grandson Asoka took over, India was already united into its first great empire.

*Chandragupta drove out the remaining Greeks and became ruler of the land Alexander had occupied.*

*Asoka sent envoys to faraway Egypt and Libya, calling on them to take up his Buddhist hopes for an end to war.*

TO EGYPT

*Harvesting mangoes*

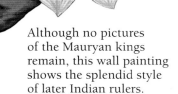

Although no pictures of the Mauryan kings remain, this wall painting shows the splendid style of later Indian rulers.

## ASOKA THE CONVERT

The Mauryan Empire reached its peak under the rule of Asoka. He came to power around 272 BC, with a reputation for war and violence. Under his leadership, the empire grew even bigger. Main roads, known as royal highways, linked the farthest corners of the country. The turning point in Asoka's life came after the Battle of Kalinga. During the bloody battle against the Kalinga army, more than 100,000 soldiers and civilians were killed. Asoka was so horrified by all the bloodshed that he converted to Buddhism. From then on, his leadership changed. He began to practice Buddha's laws of non-violence and encouraged peace between all people. He arranged for hospitals to be built and introduced plans to protect the forests.

The pillar at Sarnath was the first of many monuments erected by Asoka across the empire. The pillar was topped by four lions seated over four wheels of the law – symbols of Buddhism. The four lions were adopted as the crest of modern India.

## BUDDHA – THE ENLIGHTENED ONE

Siddhartha Gautama was born in 563 BC into a princely Indian family. When he left home, he saw so much suffering that he needed to go away and meditate on the meaning of life. In the India of that time, people believed that they were reborn many times, paying in each life for the mistakes (or being rewarded for the goodness) of the life before. After six years of study and prayer, Gautama achieved enlightenment (complete understanding) and was called the Buddha, or "enlightened one."

Buddha taught his followers how to achieve peace (nirvana) and to escape the endless cycle of rebirth. This statue shows Buddha seated on a lotus leaf.

## BUILDING SIGHTS

In his enthusiasm for Buddhism, Asoka built, and encouraged others to build, monasteries and sacred mounds, called stupas. He also erected polished sandstone pillars across the empire. The pillars were engraved with pledges to rule with kindness and truth. Craftsmen from Persia contributed to the style of the stonework. The Mauryan rulers lived in a splendid palace at Pataliputra. As there was not enough good local stone for building, the palace was made of wood from the tropical forests. The palace was set in a park with gardens, lakes, and even a race track.

The Stupa of Sanchi was built during Asoka's reign. Stupas were mound-shaped monuments built over sacred relics at places connected with the Buddha's life.

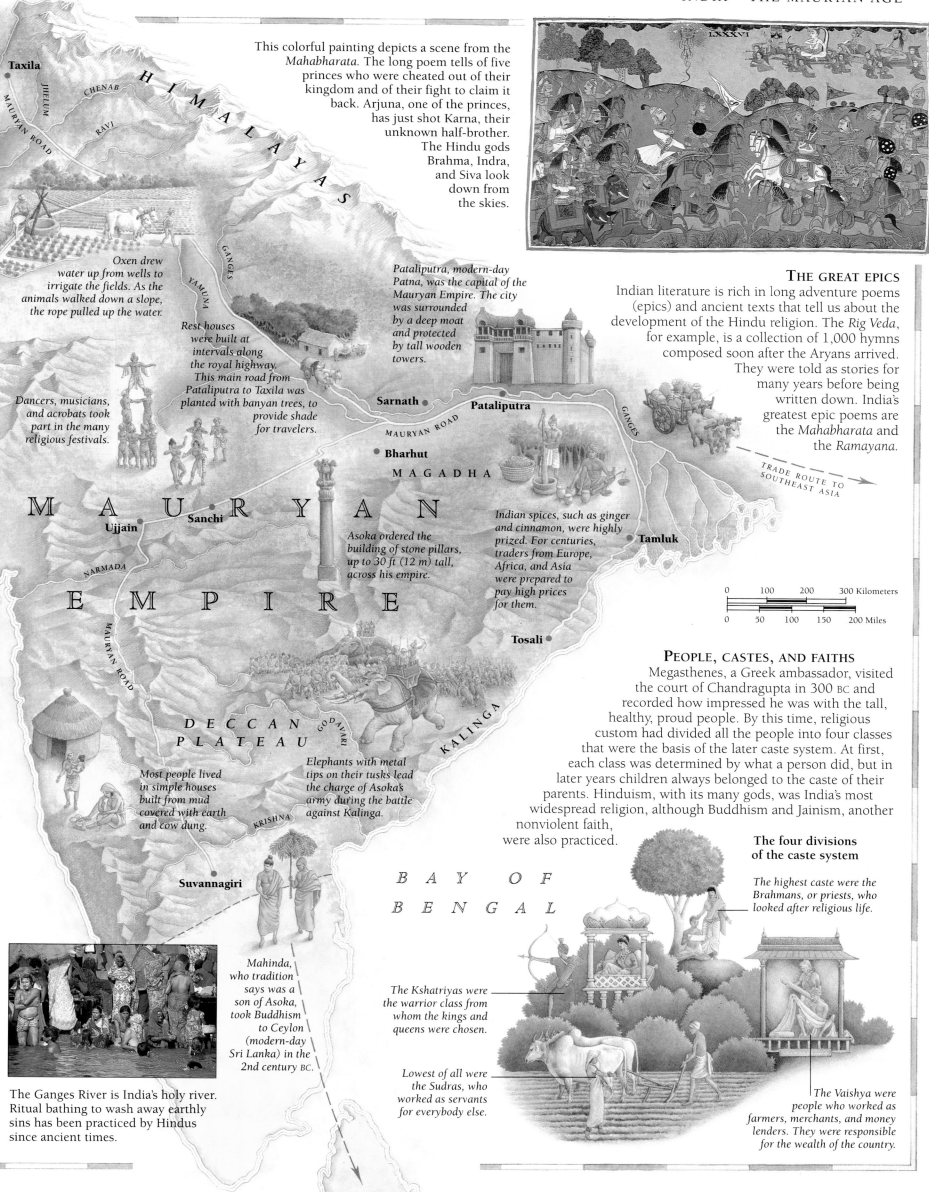

This colorful painting depicts a scene from the *Mahabharata*. The long poem tells of five princes who were cheated out of their kingdom and of their fight to claim it back. Arjuna, one of the princes, has just shot Karna, their unknown half-brother. The Hindu gods Brahma, Indra, and Siva look down from the skies.

*Oxen drew water up from wells to irrigate the fields. As the animals walked down a slope, the rope pulled up the water.*

*Rest houses were built at intervals along the royal highway. This main road from Pataliputra to Taxila was planted with banyan trees, to provide shade for travelers.*

*Dancers, musicians, and acrobats took part in the many religious festivals.*

*Pataliputra, modern-day Patna, was the capital of the Mauryan Empire. The city was surrounded by a deep moat and protected by tall wooden towers.*

Sarnath •  **Pataliputra**

• **Bharhut**

**MAGADHA**

*Asoka ordered the building of stone pillars, up to 30 ft (12 m) tall, across his empire.*

*Indian spices, such as ginger and cinnamon, were highly prized. For centuries, traders from Europe, Africa, and Asia were prepared to pay high prices for them.*

**Ujjain**   **Sanchi**

**Tamluk**

**Tosali** •

### THE GREAT EPICS

Indian literature is rich in long adventure poems (epics) and ancient texts that tell us about the development of the Hindu religion. The *Rig Veda*, for example, is a collection of 1,000 hymns composed soon after the Aryans arrived. They were told as stories for many years before being written down. India's greatest epic poems are the *Mahabharata* and the *Ramayana*.

TRADE ROUTE TO SOUTHEAST ASIA

**Taxila**

HIMALAYAS

MAURYAN ROAD

JHELUM   CHENAB   RAVI

GANGES   YAMUNA

MAURYAN ROAD

MAURYAN    EMPIRE

NARMADA

MAURYAN ROAD

**DECCAN PLATEAU**   GODAVARI

KALINGA

GANGES

| 0 | 100 | 200 | 300 Kilometers |
| 0 | 50 | 100 | 150 | 200 Miles |

### PEOPLE, CASTES, AND FAITHS

Megasthenes, a Greek ambassador, visited the court of Chandragupta in 300 BC and recorded how impressed he was with the tall, healthy, proud people. By this time, religious custom had divided all the people into four classes that were the basis of the later caste system. At first, each class was determined by what a person did, but in later years children always belonged to the caste of their parents. Hinduism, with its many gods, was India's most widespread religion, although Buddhism and Jainism, another nonviolent faith, were also practiced.

*Most people lived in simple houses built from mud covered with earth and cow dung.*

*Elephants with metal tips on their tusks lead the charge of Asoka's army during the battle against Kalinga.*

KRISHNA

**Suvannagiri**

*B A Y   O F   B E N G A L*

**The four divisions of the caste system**

*The highest caste were the Brahmans, or priests, who looked after religious life.*

*Mahinda, who tradition says was a son of Asoka, took Buddhism to Ceylon (modern-day Sri Lanka) in the 2nd century BC.*

*The Kshatriyas were the warrior class from whom the kings and queens were chosen.*

The Ganges River is India's holy river. Ritual bathing to wash away earthly sins has been practiced by Hindus since ancient times.

*Lowest of all were the Sudras, who worked as servants for everybody else.*

*The Vaishya were people who worked as farmers, merchants, and money lenders. They were responsible for the wealth of the country.*

CEYLON

47

# CHINA – THE FIRST EMPEROR

UNTIL THE YEAR 221 BC, China was divided into separate states, each with its own king. These rival kingdoms had been at war for more than 250 years. Then Cheng, who was king of the state of Ch'in (from which we get the word China), emerged as the winner. To show his superior power, Cheng gave himself the grand title Ch'in Shi Huang Ti, which means "First Ch'in Sovereign Emperor."

Cheng was determined to keep the country together. He removed the old rulers from power and forced them to live in the capital at Hsienyang. Then he divided the country into new districts with officials to see that everything was run efficiently. Cheng ordered the building of a road and canal network that would link the country. He also sent a vast task force of workers to build the Great Wall of China, parts of which still stand today. However, despite all Cheng's efforts, the empire collapsed soon after his death in 210 BC.

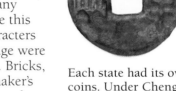

The First Emperor ordered the burning of books that did not agree with his own ideas. Scholars who objected were thrown into a pit.

### THE TIGER OF CH'IN

Cheng came to the throne of Ch'in when he was only 13 years old. He was a brilliant general and politician who would let no one get in his way. His tough character earned him the nickname the "Tiger of Ch'in." Despite this title, the Emperor was afraid of death. His grand palace had more than 1,000 bedrooms. He spent each night in a different room to confuse assassins who might try to kill him while he slept.

Weights and measures had to be standardized. This old jade weight is from the province of Ch'in.

### SETTING STANDARDS

The First Emperor needed to unite the land and rebuild its wealth after so many years of war. To make this easier, the many characters of the written language were made the same throughout the land. Bricks, like other goods, had to bear the maker's name. If the items were faulty, the maker could be punished. Even cart axles had to be the same width, so they could all use the ruts worn into the roads.

Each state had its own coins. Under Cheng, all coins were round with a hole in the center, so they could be kept on a string.

*The palace at the imperial capital*

*Windows for firing crossbows*

*The wall was 30 ft (9 m) tall and wide enough for chariots.*

*Watchtowers were built along the wall.*

*Stone slabs covered the earth and rubble.*

### THE GREAT WALL

China had long been in danger from the nomadic Hsiung Nu tribes (also called Huns), who lived to the north. Local rulers had tried to keep them out by building a series of great walls. In 214 BC, the First Emperor ordered them to be joined into one huge wall more than 2,150 miles (3,460 km) long to guard the frontier. Thousands of peasants risked their lives when they were sent to work on the wall. The weather was often wet and cold, conditions were dangerous, and men who died were buried where they fell.

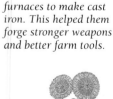

*The Chinese built blast furnaces to make cast iron. This helped them forge stronger weapons and better farm tools.*

*General Meng T'ien was responsible for building the wall. He sent officials to inspect the work.*

*Soldiers guarded against attack.*

*Peasants were forced to work on the wall.*

*An overseer held a whip.*

*Workers used simple tools, such as spades and picks, baskets and wheelbarrows, to move earth.*

*Scaffolding was made from bamboo poles tied together.*

GOBI DESERT

THE GREAT WALL

YELLOW RIVER

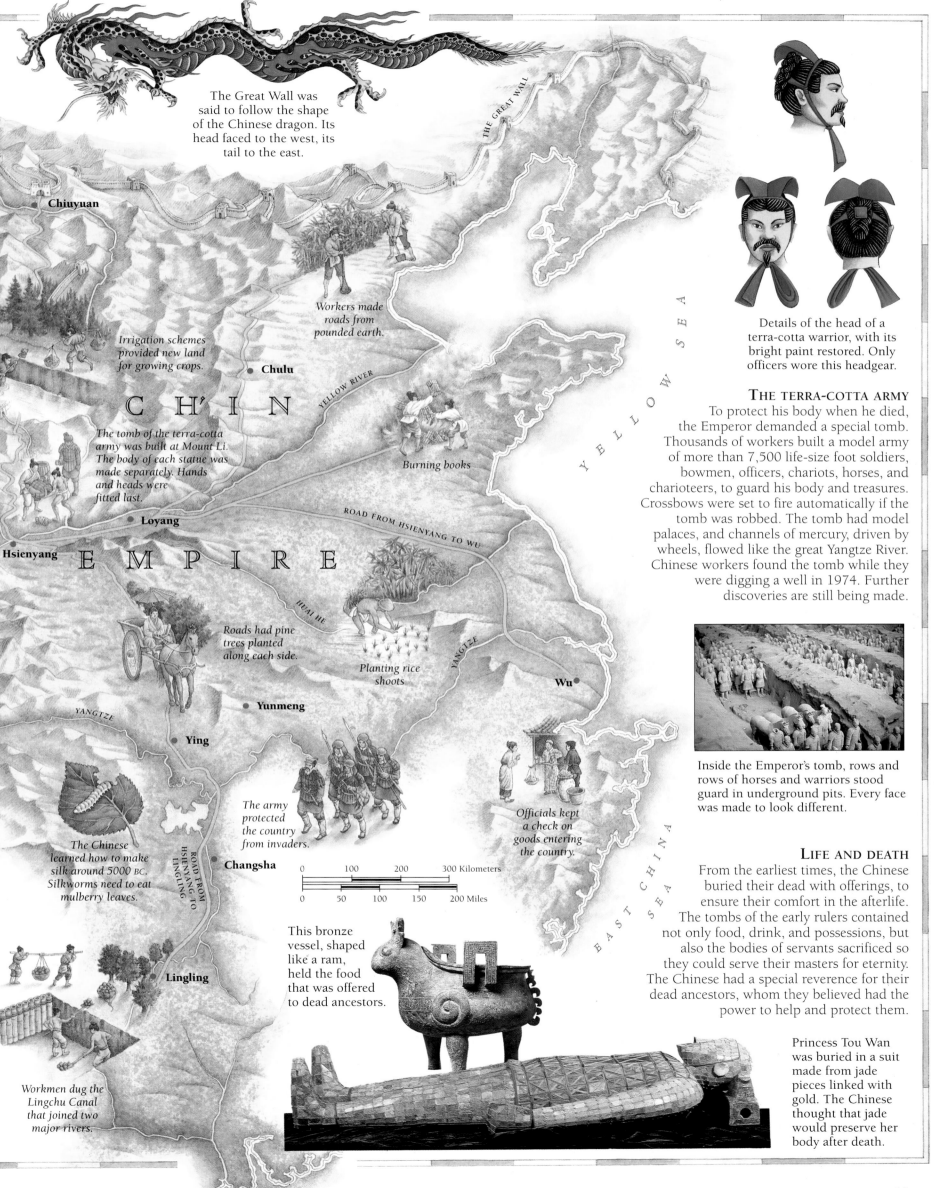

The Great Wall was said to follow the shape of the Chinese dragon. Its head faced to the west, its tail to the east.

**Chiuyuan**

Workers made roads from pounded earth.

Irrigation schemes provided new land for growing crops.

**Chulu**

C H 'I N

The tomb of the terra-cotta army was built at Mount Li. The body of each statue was made separately. Hands and heads were fitted last.

YELLOW RIVER

Burning books

**Loyang**

**Hsienyang**

E M P I R E

ROAD FROM HSIENYANG TO WU

Roads had pine trees planted along each side.

HUAI HE

Planting rice shoots

YANGTZE

**Wu**

YANGTZE

**Ying**

**Yunmeng**

The Chinese learned how to make silk around 5000 BC. Silkworms need to eat mulberry leaves.

ROAD FROM HSIENYANG TO LINGLING

The army protected the country from invaders.

**Changsha**

Officials kept a check on goods entering the country.

| 0 | 100 | 200 | 300 Kilometers |
| 0 | 50 | 100 | 150 | 200 Miles |

**Lingling**

This bronze vessel, shaped like a ram, held the food that was offered to dead ancestors.

Workmen dug the Lingchu Canal that joined two major rivers.

Details of the head of a terra-cotta warrior, with its bright paint restored. Only officers wore this headgear.

### THE TERRA-COTTA ARMY

To protect his body when he died, the Emperor demanded a special tomb. Thousands of workers built a model army of more than 7,500 life-size foot soldiers, bowmen, officers, chariots, horses, and charioteers, to guard his body and treasures. Crossbows were set to fire automatically if the tomb was robbed. The tomb had model palaces, and channels of mercury, driven by wheels, flowed like the great Yangtze River. Chinese workers found the tomb while they were digging a well in 1974. Further discoveries are still being made.

Inside the Emperor's tomb, rows and rows of horses and warriors stood guard in underground pits. Every face was made to look different.

### LIFE AND DEATH

From the earliest times, the Chinese buried their dead with offerings, to ensure their comfort in the afterlife. The tombs of the early rulers contained not only food, drink, and possessions, but also the bodies of servants sacrificed so they could serve their masters for eternity. The Chinese had a special reverence for their dead ancestors, whom they believed had the power to help and protect them.

Princess Tou Wan was buried in a suit made from jade pieces linked with gold. The Chinese thought that jade would preserve her body after death.

YELLOW SEA

EAST CHINA SEA

THE GREAT WALL

49

# NORTH AMERICAN PEOPLES

THE EARLIEST SETTLERS in North America arrived from Asia at least 20,000 years ago. At that time, the continents of Asia and America were joined by a land bridge that disappeared under the sea at the end of the last Ice Age. Groups of hunters wandered across the land, following the animals on which they lived.

These migrations were amazingly successful. The hunter-gatherers spread out and populated North and South America – a vast area of widely varying temperatures and landscapes. The Native Americans – the name these people are known by in modern times, after being mistakenly named Indians by early explorers – learned to live in mountains and plains, forests and deserts, marshes, and frozen wastes. Some became farmers, while others lived in villages or large towns. Many remained hunter-gatherers, living off the rich variety of food they found on the land.

*In summer, northern hunters lived in tents of caribou hide. Women prepared the caribou skin, men decorated the antlers using a bow drill.*

*Fishermen hunted the rivers, especially at rapids, and caught salmon using 10 ft (3 m) spears.*

*This hunter is disguised as a caribou to help him get close to the herd.*

## HUNTERS OF THE NORTH

In the bitter cold of the far north, the Inuit (also known as Eskimos), adapted to the frozen land and sea. They hunted all the Arctic animals, birds, and fish, but their main supplies of food and clothing came from seals and caribou. In winter, when the Inuit traveled in search of food, they lived in temporary homes made from blocks of hard-packed snow. Some of these homes, called igloos, had several rooms. The Inuit also built cabins of stone, turf, and timber, or lived in tents.

*The Makah people of Ozette were expert whale hunters. They harpooned whales from huge dugout canoes. One whale would supply the village with meat, oil, and bones for tools.*

## NATIVE AMERICANS OF THE PLAINS

The lands of the Plains tribes (which had names such as Blackfoot, Crow, and Dakota) stretched from the Rocky Mountains to the Mississippi valley. The Great Plains were rich in wildlife, with deer, wolves, and herds of buffalo. But most people lived on the fringes of the Plains and along the Missouri River. They planted crops in spring, gathered wild fruits in summer, and harvested in the autumn. Once or twice a year they hunted the buffalo that provided hide for clothes and teepees and food for the winter months.

Many tribes lived in teepees, tents made from buffalo hide.

*Acorns were an important food. They were shelled, dried, and pounded into flour. This was soaked to remove the tannic acid before being made into cakes.*

## THE MOUND BUILDERS

In about AD 200, a group of people we call the Hopewell replaced the Adena in the Ohio River valley. They are known as mound builders because they buried their dead under great mounds of earth up to 40 ft (12 m) high and made shapes in the earth, like the Great Serpent Mound. The Hopewell were energetic traders who brought goods from as far away as the Rocky Mountains, the Great Lakes, the Gulf of Mexico, and the far north. They were also talented craftworkers who made fine pottery. For reasons that are unclear, the culture had disappeared by AD 550.

This Hopewell hand was cut from mica, a kind of mineral found in the mountains. It was designed as a grave offering.

*Pueblo peoples dug irrigation systems to water their crops of corn, beans, and squash.*

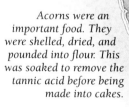

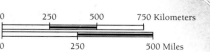

| 0 | 250 | 500 | 750 Kilometers |
| 0 | | 250 | 500 Miles |

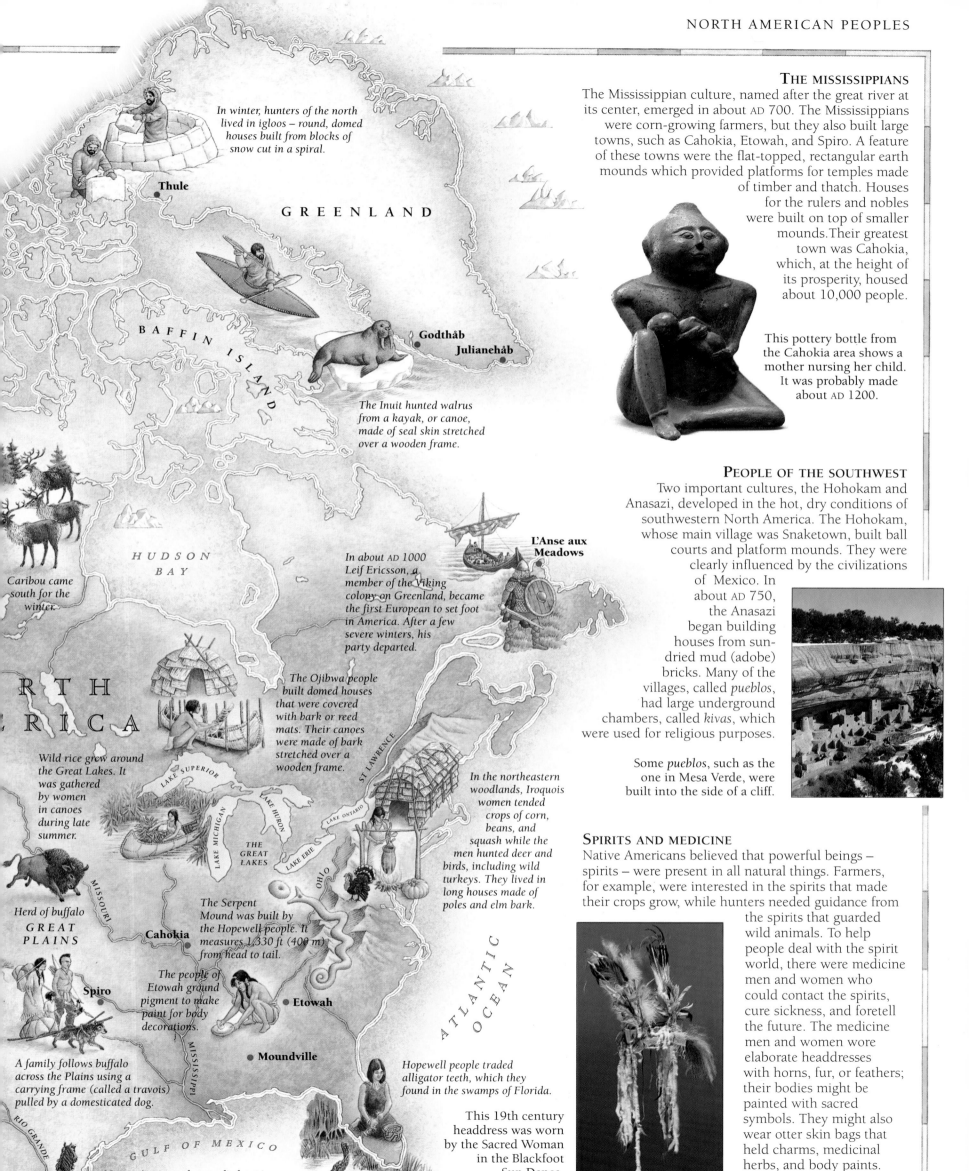

*In winter, hunters of the north lived in igloos – round, domed houses built from blocks of snow cut in a spiral.*

**Thule**

GREENLAND

BAFFIN ISLAND

**Godthåb**
**Julianehåb**

*The Inuit hunted walrus from a kayak, or canoe, made of seal skin stretched over a wooden frame.*

HUDSON BAY

*Caribou came south for the winter.*

*In about AD 1000 Leif Ericsson, a member of the Viking colony on Greenland, became the first European to set foot in America. After a few severe winters, his party departed.*

**L'Anse aux Meadows**

*The Ojibwa people built domed houses that were covered with bark or reed mats. Their canoes were made of bark stretched over a wooden frame.*

RTH
RICA

*Wild rice grew around the Great Lakes. It was gathered by women in canoes during late summer.*

LAKE SUPERIOR

LAKE MICHIGAN

LAKE HURON

THE GREAT LAKES

LAKE ONTARIO

LAKE ERIE

ST LAWRENCE

OHIO

*In the northeastern woodlands, Iroquois women tended crops of corn, beans, and squash while the men hunted deer and birds, including wild turkeys. They lived in long houses made of poles and elm bark.*

MISSOURI

*Herd of buffalo*
GREAT PLAINS

**Cahokia**

*The Serpent Mound was built by the Hopewell people. It measures 1,330 ft (400 m) from head to tail.*

**Spiro**

*The people of Etowah ground pigment to make paint for body decorations.*

**Etowah**

ATLANTIC OCEAN

*A family follows buffalo across the Plains using a carrying frame (called a travois) pulled by a domesticated dog.*

MISSISSIPPI

**Moundville**

RIO GRANDE

GULF OF MEXICO

*Hopewell people traded alligator teeth, which they found in the swamps of Florida.*

*This 19th century headdress was worn by the Sacred Woman in the Blackfoot Sun Dance.*

*Native American horses died out in prehistoric times. When the Spanish arrived in Central America in the 1500s, they brought horses with them. Some of them escaped and reached the Great Plains.*

### THE MISSISSIPPIANS

The Mississippian culture, named after the great river at its center, emerged in about AD 700. The Mississippians were corn-growing farmers, but they also built large towns, such as Cahokia, Etowah, and Spiro. A feature of these towns were the flat-topped, rectangular earth mounds which provided platforms for temples made of timber and thatch. Houses for the rulers and nobles were built on top of smaller mounds. Their greatest town was Cahokia, which, at the height of its prosperity, housed about 10,000 people.

*This pottery bottle from the Cahokia area shows a mother nursing her child. It was probably made about AD 1200.*

### PEOPLE OF THE SOUTHWEST

Two important cultures, the Hohokam and Anasazi, developed in the hot, dry conditions of southwestern North America. The Hohokam, whose main village was Snaketown, built ball courts and platform mounds. They were clearly influenced by the civilizations of Mexico. In about AD 750, the Anasazi began building houses from sun-dried mud (adobe) bricks. Many of the villages, called *pueblos*, had large underground chambers, called *kivas*, which were used for religious purposes.

*Some pueblos, such as the one in Mesa Verde, were built into the side of a cliff.*

### SPIRITS AND MEDICINE

Native Americans believed that powerful beings – spirits – were present in all natural things. Farmers, for example, were interested in the spirits that made their crops grow, while hunters needed guidance from the spirits that guarded wild animals. To help people deal with the spirit world, there were medicine men and women who could contact the spirits, cure sickness, and foretell the future. The medicine men and women wore elaborate headdresses with horns, fur, or feathers; their bodies might be painted with sacred symbols. They might also wear otter skin bags that held charms, medicinal herbs, and body paints.

# THE FIRST AUSTRALIANS

THE FIRST AUSTRALIANS were nomadic people who arrived from Southeast Asia about 40,000 years ago across land that is now submerged. They originally settled around the fertile coasts and rivers but later moved across the continent, adapting to areas of rain forest, mountains, and desert. In desert areas, people lived in small groups, often moving camp in search of food. In more fertile areas, they built homes that could be used for several months.

These original inhabitants were later called "Aboriginals," meaning people who had lived there since the earliest times. Because there were no wheeled vehicles or animals, the Aboriginals walked everywhere. Each group traveled along familiar paths within its own territory. Many of these routes were thought to be the paths of their Dreamtime ancestors.

Aboriginals in modern-day Australia still perform special dances as part of ceremonies to re-enact their ancestral past.

*People in Arnhem Land built huts on raised platforms. Fires were lit underneath to keep mosquitoes away. Dogs called dingoes guarded the camp.*

ARNHEM LAND

*Along the northeast coast, people hunted turtles from outrigger canoes. They also gathered turtle eggs from the beaches.*

*Dancers decorated their bodies with white, red, or yellow designs, usually in circles and lines. Music was played on a didgeridoo.*

*Dreamtime stories were often told with drawings on the ground. Most images were not allowed to be seen by strangers. The design drawn here was for an open ceremony.*

CORAL SEA

*An emu was lured into a trap by a man playing a wooden horn.*

AUSTRALIA

*Hunters caught kangaroos with returning sticks (boomerangs) or spears. Men often smeared themselves with mud so the animals could not smell them approaching.*

*Uluru, also known as Ayers Rock, has always been a sacred place for the Aboriginals.*

*A man drinks water from a well he has dug. A woman uses a stone to grind grass seeds she has collected.*

*Men used nets to catch fish in the Murray and Darling rivers. They also used nets and traps to catch waterfowl, shellfish, and platypus.*

DARLING

LACHLAN

MURRAY

MURRAY

*Women used digging sticks to find yams, an edible root. They were collected in a wooden dish and carried back to camp.*

SOUTHERN OCEAN

*A woman beats fiber from tree bark before spinning it into string. The string was woven into a dilly bag used for collecting food. In winter people wore cloaks made of possum skins.*

## DREAMTIME ANCESTORS

The Aboriginals believe that in the beginning, ancestral heroes wandered the earth and gave it meaning. This was known as the Dreamtime, or *Tjukurpa*. Some ancestors were human, others were animals and plants, sun, wind, and rain. Ancestors moved around the land following certain paths. These paths were important because they linked the land and the people. By looking after the sacred sites and re-enacting the actions of the ancestors, Aboriginals can be sure of continuing harmony in their world.

Many Aboriginal cave paintings show the ancestral heroes and their adventures in the Dreamtime.

*People dug channels so that eels would swim inland. They were then caught and eaten.*

## THE GOOD EARTH

Aboriginal people lived off the land but did not cultivate it at all. Most of their time was spent finding food. Women searched for edible roots, grass seeds, grubs, and small animals such as lizards. Men hunted larger animals such as kangaroos and possum, or caught fish and ducks from the rivers and coasts. People knew which trees to climb to find honey and birds' eggs. Trees also provided berries and nuts, as well as wood for boats, spears, shields, and dishes, and branches that could be used for shelters.

TASMAN SEA

TASMANIA

*On the island of Tasmania, women collected seashells which could be traded for items they needed.*

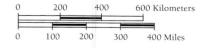

| 0 | | 200 | | 400 | | 600 Kilometers |
|---|---|---|---|---|---|---|

| 0 | 100 | 200 | 300 | 400 Miles |
|---|---|---|---|---|

# POLYNESIA AND NEW ZEALAND

STEERING BY THE SUN AND STARS, and using their knowledge of the sea, the Polynesians settled most of the islands in the vast Pacific Ocean. To cross great expanses of open sea, these skilled seafarers studied wind and wave patterns, interpreted cloud formations, and watched the behavior of certain land-based birds. Historians think that people originally set out from the islands of Southeast Asia about 4,000 years ago. Tonga and Samoa were settled first, then the Marquesas Islands and Tahiti. From there, some sailors explored northward, reaching Hawaii by about AD 100. Others headed east to Pitcairn and still more reached Easter Island by about AD 400. Although the way of life varied slightly from one group of islands to another, most early Polynesians lived in small communities grouped into tribes ruled by powerful chiefs. The last great journey, in about AD 950, was undertaken by a group of Polynesians to a land they called Aotearoa – now New Zealand.

*Sails made from palm-leaf matting*

*Coconut palm provided fiber for rope*

*Sheltered area for food supplies*

*Hull made from tree trunk*

HAWAIIAN ISLANDS

*Across the Hawaiian Islands people built stone temples called heiau with wickerwork structures to represent their gods.*

## OCEAN TRAVEL
The early Polynesians used their boats for fishing, trading, and for long journeys to planned destinations or to explore. The most common boats in the islands were canoes, which were built in many shapes and sizes. They could carry one person or be 100 ft (30 m) long and capable of transporting up to 500 people over distances of more than 1,500 miles (2,500 km). Paddles were used for covering short distances but sails were needed to catch the wind for long journeys.

LINE ISLANDS

CHRISTMAS ISLAND

*Dancers were accompanied by musicians playing drums, bamboo flutes, or shells.*

This carved figure from Hawaii shows a local volcano goddess, Pele. The Hawaiian Islands are formed from a chain of old volcanoes. The Polynesians who lived there believed that Pele could melt rocks and make mountains.

TUVALU

*PACIFIC OCEAN*

SAMOA

*Women wove baskets from the fronds of the coconut palm. The trunk provided timber for homes, and the leaves were used for thatch. The coconut itself was a source of food and drink.*

MARQUESAS ISLANDS

SOCIETY ISLANDS

*Early colonists set out from Tonga and Samoa with men, women, children, animals, and seeds for planting crammed into their canoes.*

TONGA

COOK ISLANDS

TAHITI

*Later Polynesians started to grow sweet potatoes, taro, bananas, and breadfruit, and kept dogs, pigs, and chickens.*

*Two Maori warriors fight in a duel. Each man used a sharp-edged club made of whalebone or a type of jade called greenstone.*

*Islanders ate mainly seafood, yams, and fruit. Leaves were used as plates and often still are for feasts. Fish were caught by spear, net, or even by hand.*

*Pigs were sometimes sacrificed and placed on platforms as an offering to the gods.*

PITCAIRN

EASTER ISLAND

NEW ZEALAND

SOUTH ISLAND

NORTH ISLAND

CHATHAM ISLAND

*Maori chiefs often had a pattern of tattoo marks carved on their faces. They wore cloaks of woven flax and kiwi feathers.*

## THE LARGEST ISLANDS
When the Polynesians (who were later called Maoris) reached New Zealand, they found the land was much colder and wetter than they were used to. The only familiar crop they could grow was a type of sweet potato. They hunted a large flightless bird, the moa, and relied on farming, fishing, and gathering. Maori families belonged to a tribe and were ruled by a chief, or *rangatiri*. They worshiped the spirits of dead ancestors and also believed that certain people or places were sacred. These were called called *tapu*, or taboo.

*Small canoes were used to travel between neighboring islands.*

The Maoris were expert woodcarvers. This sculpture shows one of their main ancestors, Pukaki, with his two sons.

*From AD 1100 onward, the people of Easter Island set up great stone statues up to 30 ft (10 m) tall.*

| 0 | 500 | 1000 | 1500 Kilometers |
|---|---|---|---|
| 0 | | 500 | 1000 Miles |

# CHINA – THE GOLDEN AGE

CHINA HAD BEEN through many years of war following the death of the First Emperor. But by AD 626, under the rule of the young Emperor T'ang T'ai-tsung, the country settled into a new and golden age. The capital city, now at Ch'angan, became the center for traders who arrived on the Silk Road.

Markets and bazaars buzzed with activity, and many kinds of religion existed side by side. For the first time, people – not just the rich – could get good government jobs. The production of salt, paper, and iron also provided work. During this peaceful time, arts and crafts flourished.

The shape of these hills in southern China made a favorite subject for painters.

In AD 751 the Muslim forces defeated the Chinese at the Battle of Talas. The Chinese lost control of the Kashgar area..

Nomadic tribes on the northern frontier were a constant threat and had to be watched.

THE SILK ROAD

**Tashkent**

**Kucha**

Camel caravans headed west along the Silk Road, named for the important trade in silk.

**Samarkand**

In AD 629, the Chinese monk Hsüan Tsang returned from India with Buddhist texts for his fellow students.

**Kashgar**

Traders and their animals traveled in groups called caravans. They rested overnight during the long journey along the Silk Road.

T' A N G

THE SILK ROAD

**Khotan**

## THE GOOD LIFE

The wealthy people of China lead a very comfortable life. They wore beautiful silk clothes and entertained their friends with lavish feasts. Servants prepared meals of roasted pig and deer, which were washed down with drinks made from millet and rice. In their spare time, they listened to music and poetry and played games such as chess and cards. People filled their homes with luxury goods made of gold and silver, jade, and porcelain. Lacquerwork and paintings on silk were also very popular.

This elegant model of a court lady shows how wealthy women of the time would have dressed.

| 0 | 100 | 200 | 300 | 400 Kilometers |
| 0 | 100 | 200 | | 300 Miles |

TRADE ROUTE TO INDIA

## GREAT INVENTIONS

The Chinese were brilliant inventors. By the time of the T'ang emperors, they could make paper, and later they discovered how to print on paper using blocks of wood. They also designed a device to detect the earthquakes that sometimes hit China. During the T'ang dynasty, they invented a mechanical water clock, the first magnetic compass, paper playing cards, and the fine porcelain that we still call "china."

This scene is from the world's oldest printed book, known as the Diamond Sutra. It was printed in AD 868.

## THE CAPITAL OF CH'ANGAN

Under the T'ang emperors, the capital at Ch'angan became the largest city in the world. The name Ch'angan means "Forever Safe." The city had a population of more than one million people, as well as many foreign traders, scholars, and travelers.

The emperor's palace was built in the northern area of the city and was surrounded by a high wall.

Peasant farmers had to spend time in the army.

Musicians and dancers performed in the town square.

Buildings were made from wood covered with lacquer. Roofs were tiled.

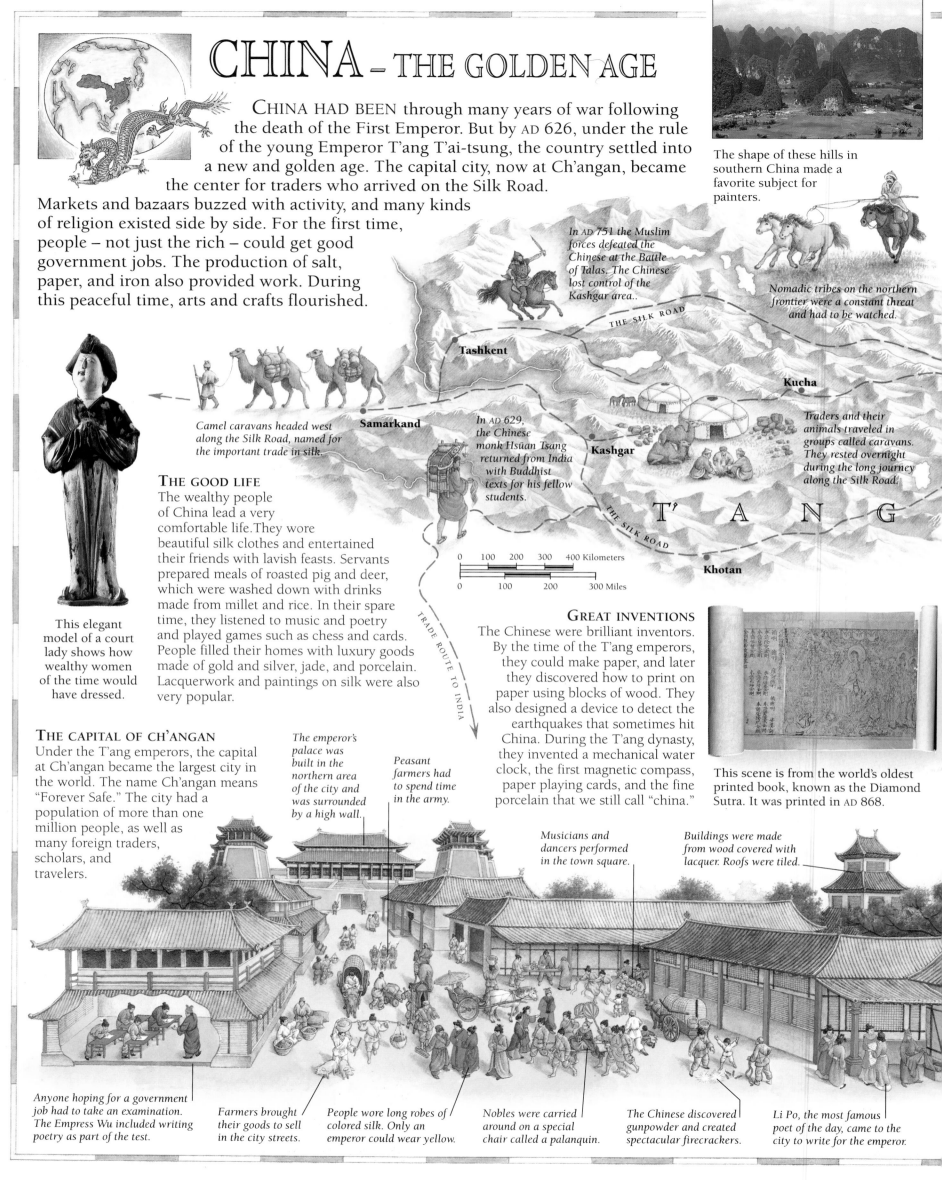

Anyone hoping for a government job had to take an examination. The Empress Wu included writing poetry as part of the test.

Farmers brought their goods to sell in the city streets.

People wore long robes of colored silk. Only an emperor could wear yellow.

Nobles were carried around on a special chair called a palanquin.

The Chinese discovered gunpowder and created spectacular firecrackers.

Li Po, the most famous poet of the day, came to the city to write for the emperor.

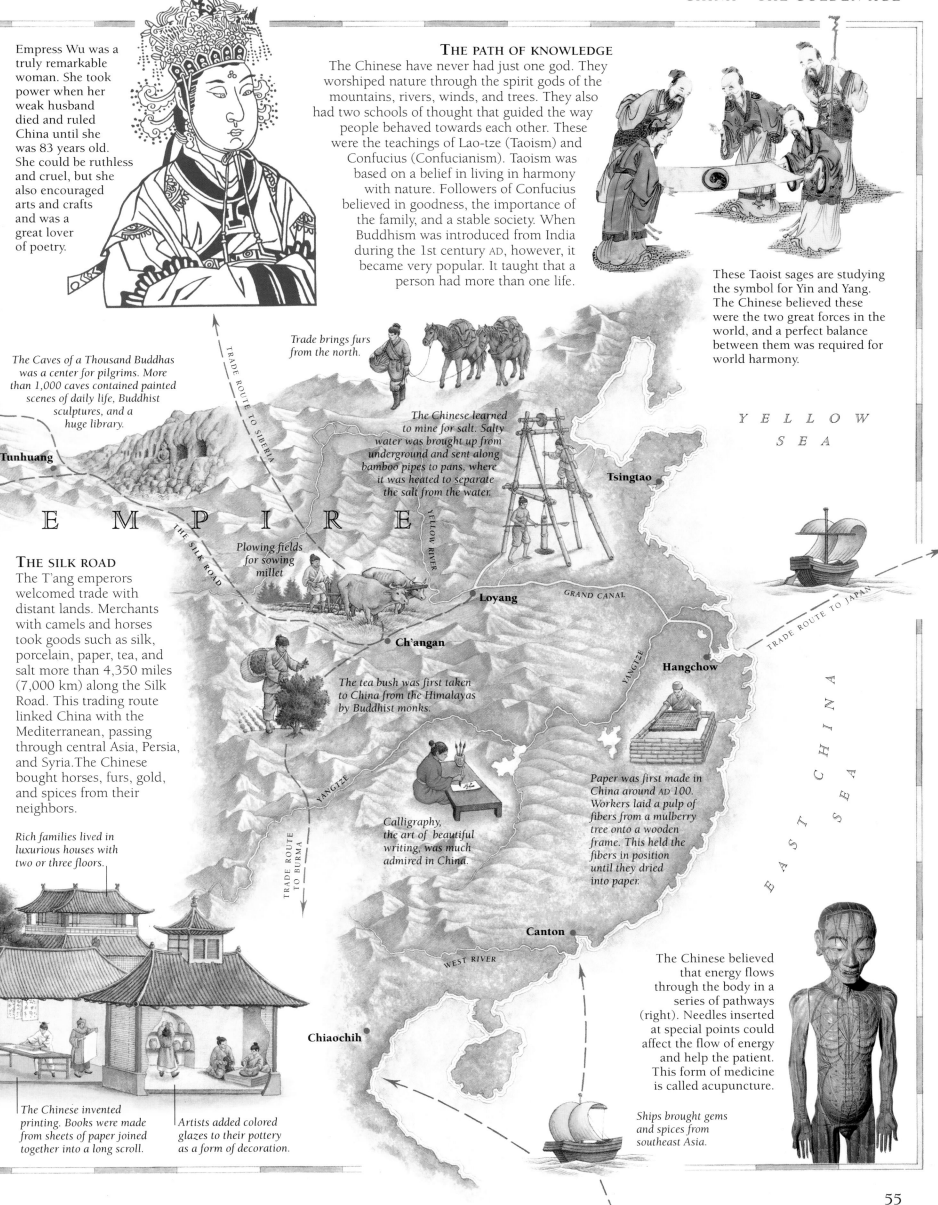

Empress Wu was a truly remarkable woman. She took power when her weak husband died and ruled China until she was 83 years old. She could be ruthless and cruel, but she also encouraged arts and crafts and was a great lover of poetry.

## THE PATH OF KNOWLEDGE

The Chinese have never had just one god. They worshiped nature through the spirit gods of the mountains, rivers, winds, and trees. They also had two schools of thought that guided the way people behaved towards each other. These were the teachings of Lao-tze (Taoism) and Confucius (Confucianism). Taoism was based on a belief in living in harmony with nature. Followers of Confucius believed in goodness, the importance of the family, and a stable society. When Buddhism was introduced from India during the 1st century AD, however, it became very popular. It taught that a person had more than one life.

These Taoist sages are studying the symbol for Yin and Yang. The Chinese believed these were the two great forces in the world, and a perfect balance between them was required for world harmony.

*The Caves of a Thousand Buddhas was a center for pilgrims. More than 1,000 caves contained painted scenes of daily life, Buddhist sculptures, and a huge library.*

**Tunhuang**

*Trade brings furs from the north.*

TRADE ROUTE TO SIBERIA

*The Chinese learned to mine for salt. Salty water was brought up from underground and sent along bamboo pipes to pans, where it was heated to separate the salt from the water.*

**Tsingtao**

Y E L L O W  S E A

E M P I R E

THE SILK ROAD

## THE SILK ROAD

The T'ang emperors welcomed trade with distant lands. Merchants with camels and horses took goods such as silk, porcelain, paper, tea, and salt more than 4,350 miles (7,000 km) along the Silk Road. This trading route linked China with the Mediterranean, passing through central Asia, Persia, and Syria. The Chinese bought horses, furs, gold, and spices from their neighbors.

*Plowing fields for sowing millet*

YELLOW RIVER

**Loyang**

GRAND CANAL

**Ch'angan**

*The tea bush was first taken to China from the Himalayas by Buddhist monks.*

YANGTZE

**Hangchow**

TRADE ROUTE TO JAPAN

*Rich families lived in luxurious houses with two or three floors.*

YANGTZE

TRADE ROUTE TO BURMA

*Calligraphy, the art of beautiful writing, was much admired in China.*

*Paper was first made in China around AD 100. Workers laid a pulp of fibers from a mulberry tree onto a wooden frame. This held the fibers in position until they dried into paper.*

E A S T  C H I N A  S E A

**Canton**

WEST RIVER

**Chiaochih**

*The Chinese invented printing. Books were made from sheets of paper joined together into a long scroll.*

*Artists added colored glazes to their pottery as a form of decoration.*

The Chinese believed that energy flows through the body in a series of pathways (right). Needles inserted at special points could affect the flow of energy and help the patient. This form of medicine is called acupuncture.

*Ships brought gems and spices from southeast Asia.*

# JAPAN – RISE OF THE SAMURAI

THE FIRST EMPEROR OF JAPAN was the legendary Jimmu Tenno, who was said to be descended from the Sun Goddess. At first the emperors of Japan ruled alone. They owned all the land and kept order with an army of peasant soldiers. But during the Heian Period (AD 794-1185), the emperors gave much land away to noble families, called clans. These clans gradually became rich enough to set up their own armies.

In AD 858 the powerful Fujiwara clan, while still respecting the emperor, took control of the government. For a time they ruled efficiently, but other clans challenged the Fujiwaras. In AD 1192, the Minamoto clan took over, and the emperor appointed Minamoto Yoritomo as the first shogun, or military dictator. During shogun rule, a class of warriors called samurai gained considerable power. For the next 700 years, Japan was ruled by shoguns and samurai.

## THE FLOWERING OF JAPAN

During the 6th century AD, Japan began to absorb ideas from its neighbor, China. Signs of these changes could be seen in the arts and architecture. Bronze statues of the Buddha appeared, although the national religion of Shinto remained popular. Chinese-style houses with tiled roofs were built, and Chinese writing was adapted to create a new written language. Gradually all these new ideas were changed to suit Japanese taste, producing a distinctive Japanese culture.

*This wooden figure was made during the Heian period. It shows a god known as The Immovable King of Light.*

*Chinese envoys, craftworkers, and Buddhist monks crossed to Japan.*

*Izumi was one of many Shinto shrines dedicated to the Sun Goddess.*

*Lady Murasaki Shikibu wrote the "Tale of Genji" in AD 1007. The book is more than 600,000 words long and is one of the world's first novels.*

*The early inhabitants of Japan were called the Ainu. The women performed a crane dance designed to weave a charm that would keep bears away.*

HOKKAIDO

*PACIFIC OCEAN*

*Whales were hunted as an important source of food.*

*In the 8th century AD, an imperial decree announced that the arrival of the cherry blossom be celebrated each spring.*

SEA OF JAPAN

Akita

*Rice has been an important crop in Japan since the Yayoi culture of 300 BC. It was harvested and stored above ground in granaries.*

J A P A N

HONSHU

*Fujisan – Mount Fuji – is the sacred mountain of Japan.*

Izumo

Heian-kyo (Kyoto)

Nara

SHIKOKU

Kamakura

*Minamoto Yoritomo fought the powerful Taira clan in the Gempei War (AD 1180-1185). In AD 1192, he was made shogun, the emperor's chief of military affairs.*

KYUSHU

Satsuma

*Houses were made of light wood. They could easily be rebuilt if damaged by the earthquakes that often hit Japan.*

PACIFIC OCEAN

*Nara, the first capital of Japan, was the site of the Buddhist temple of Horyu-ji. The temple was founded in AD 607.*

*Divers searched for pearls in the Pacific Ocean.*

## THE WAY OF THE WARRIOR

Japanese warriors called samurai rose to fame during the troubled 10th and 11th centuries. They protected the lands of the *daimyo* (local lords) and had a strict code of honor known as *bushido*, meaning "way of the warrior." At the beginning of a battle, each samurai proudly announced his name and those of his ancestors, challenging an opponent to come and fight him. They fought bravely and preferred to die rather than accept defeat. All samurai had to be expert horsemen, able to shoot arrows accurately from a fast-moving horse.

*The bow and arrow was the chief weapon of the early samurai.*

### Early samurai warrior

*Samurai wore helmets in battle.*

*Armor was made from strips of tough leather.*

*The best horses were from the mountains of northern Japan.*

*Swords were made from high-quality steel.*

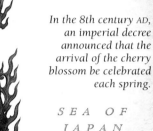

## THE COURT AT KYOTO

In AD 794 the Japanese capital moved from Nara to Heian-kyo (later called Kyoto). In the magnificent setting, the courtiers, who were known as "dwellers among the clouds," became cut off from the problems of the world outside. They lived in luxury and spent their days with dressing up, walking in the gardens, collecting beautiful objects, writing letters and poems, and attending court and temple ceremonies.

| 0 | 100 | 200 | 300 Kilometers |
|---|-----|-----|----------------|
| 0 | 50 | 100 | 150 | 200 Miles |

# KINGDOM OF THE KHMERS

THE TEMPLE CITIES of Angkor dominated the plain where the people known as Khmers flourished for more than 600 years. The Khmer kingdom, in modern-day Cambodia (Kampuchea), first rose to power under King Jayavarman II, who ruled from AD 802-850.

After years of trading with India, the Khmers adopted many aspects of Indian culture, especially the Hindu religion and Indian architecture.

Once Jayavarman was in control, he proclaimed himself a god-king with power bestowed on him by the Hindu god, Siva. From then on Khmer kings could command the loyalty of their people. They embarked on massive programs to build temples for their gods and fine palaces for themselves. Life for most Khmers was devoted to serving the god-king. Engineers built a sophisticated system of irrigation so that farmers could grow enough to feed the priests, courtiers, and craftworkers who lived in and around the enormous temple palaces.

This huge stone head shows one of the four faces of Jayavarman VII (AD 1181-1218). Jayavarman drove out the invading Chams and rebuilt the city of Angkor. Unlike other Khmer kings, he was a Buddhist, not a Hindu.

*In AD 1431 the Siamese invaded Cambodia and sacked Angkor Wat. This marked the end of the empire, and the Khmers retreated south to Phnom Penh.*

ANNAM

MEKONG

MUN

SIAM

CHAO PHRAYA

*The king appeared twice a day at a golden window, to conduct business and to hear people's complaints.*

● Koh Ker

KHMER KINGDOM

Angkor ●
● Roluos
TONLE SAP
● Preah Khan

*When the Tonle Sap lake flooded each year, men could scoop up baskets full of fish. Many families lived in stilted thatch homes around the lake.*

*Elephants were used to move heavy loads as well as for hunting.*

CHAMPA

Binh Dinh ●

SOUTH CHINA SEA

*The figures of celestial dancers, called apsaras, were carved into the walls of Angkor Wat as permanent entertainment for the gods.*

*Buddhism did not become popular until the 12th century AD.*

GULF OF SIAM

*Indravarman I organized an elaborate network of reservoirs that held water for irrigating the rice fields.*

MEKONG

Phnom Penh ●

*In AD 1177 the Chams launched a surprise attack by sailing up the Mekong River to Angkor. They were later driven out by King Jayavarman VII.*

*A Chinese envoy, Chou Ta-kuan, sailed to Angkor in AD 1296 and wrote detailed descriptions of what he saw.*

| 0 | 50 | 100 | 150 Kilometers |
| 0 | 50 | 100 Miles | |

*The feathers of peacocks and kingfishers were highly prized for their color.*

Saigon ●

● Oc Eo

FUNAN

*Scholars wrote on sections of palm leaf.*

## WATERS OF LIFE

Water played a vital role in the life of the Khmers. From May to October each year, the monsoon rains caused the Mekong River to flood and deposit silt on the land. When the waters receded, the fertile plain was used to grow rice. Rainwater was also stored in reservoirs and canals and used to irrigate the fields during the rest of the year. Water was also needed because the weather was extremely hot and people liked to bathe several times a day. Archaeologists have found the remains of several palace bathing pools.

The *naga* was a mythical snake, based on the cobra of Hindu mythology, that represented the kindly, life-giving spirit of the water.

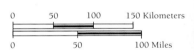

## ANGKOR WAT

Angkor Wat, meaning city temple, was a combination of temples and palaces where the god-kings lived and where they were buried before rejoining the gods. It was built by Suryavarman II in AD 1113. The buildings were made of stone and brick and were decorated with relief sculptures showing mythical scenes of Hindu gods, the Khmers at war, and great royal processions. Angkor Wat was surrounded by a massive moat and the causeway leading to the entrance of the temple was lined with images of seven-headed *nagas*.

The temple of Angkor Wat was uncovered in 1861 by French naturalist Henri Mouhot. Earlier visitors had already reported stories of seeing a "lost city" in the jungle.

# MAYA – CITIES OF STONE

THE RUINS of spectacular stone cities rise above the tropical forests of Meso (middle) America. Royal cities such as Tikal, Palenque, and Copán were home to people known as the Maya, who were at their most creative between AD 250-900. The lands of the Maya were divided into several kingdoms, each ruled by a godlike king. Every kingdom had a capital city that controlled the towns, villages, and farmlands around it.

Farmers grew corn, beans, and squash, and hunters trapped rabbit, iguana, and deer.

To impress their subjects and fellow rulers, kings enriched their cities with spectacular monuments decorated with elaborate carvings and paintings. The Maya were also clever astronomers and mathematicians. They developed a sophisticated calendar and method of counting. The Maya invented a system of writing using picture signs called glyphs that tell us about Maya kings and their conquests.

## CARVED IN STONE

The cities of the Maya were vast complexes with multistorey buildings, temple-topped pyramids, and ball courts, grouped around a central plaza. Construction of the cities must have been quite a task – the Maya had no metal for tools until later. Builders used obsidian, a rock from the solid lava of the volcanoes in the region, to carve the limestone blocks. Artists used a local red dye for decoration.

These ruins form part of the palace at Palenque, one of the cities of the Maya.

*People from the coast collected sea salt at the end of the dry season. It was traded throughout the Maya lands.*

*Women wove cotton on a backstrap loom that they carried from place to place.*

*The Olmecs (1200-400 BC) carved huge stone heads of their rulers. This one was found near the old Olmec capital of La Venta.*

**La Venta**

**GRIJALVA**

## PLAYING BALL

A fast ball game was first played by ancestors of the Maya, the Olmecs. Special courts were built for the game in the main ceremonial centers of each city. Players wore protective clothing and competed to score points by hitting a solid rubber ball without using their hands. One aim was to get the ball through one of the stone rings at either side of the court. It was not a simple sport but a religious event, and some players may have been sacrificed at the end of the game.

*Only men took part in the ball games. They used a ball made of hard rubber.*

**GULF OF MEXICO**

*Chichén Itzá was one of the later Maya cities built between AD 900-1200. The building in the foreground is thought to have been an observatory.*

**Mayapán**  **Cobá**

**Chichén Itzá**

*When farmers wanted more land for growing crops, they burned down small areas of forest. The ash enriched the soil.*

**YUCATAN PENINSULA**

**CARIBBEAN SEA**

**LAND OF THE MAYA**

**El Mirador**

**Palenque**

**Tikal**

*A woman passes a string with thorns tied in it through a cut in her tongue. The blood was considered a precious offering to the gods.*

**Yaxchilán**

**USUMACINTA**

*The jaguar was regarded as a symbol of power.*

**SIERRA MADRE DEL SUR**

**MOTAGUA**

**Copán**

*Archaeologists found the burial place of a Maya lord in the stepped pyramid at Copán.*

**PACIFIC OCEAN**

This section of stone from a temple at Yaxchilán shows Maya glyphs. Experts can "read" the dates of different rulers from these glyphs.

## MARKING TIME

The Maya were great astronomers. They used their observation of the skies to make their solar calendar, which was remarkably accurate. The solar year had 365 days, divided into 18 "months" of 20 days each – plus five unlucky days at the end of each year. There was a second calendar, for religious purposes, made up of 260 days. Only priests could read this calendar, so people consulted them before important events.

*Certain types of seashell, such as the conch, were highly prized. They were traded across the whole country.*

### MAP OF MESO (MIDDLE) AMERICA AD 250-1500

**MEXICO**

**GULF OF MEXICO**

**Teotihuacán**
**Tenochtitlán**  **LAKE TEXCOCO**

**Chichén Itzá**

**YUCATAN PENINSULA**

**Palenque**

**PACIFIC OCEAN**

**Copán**

**CENTRAL AMERICA**

- Land of the Maya
- Aztec Empire

Scale:
0   50   100   150 Kilometers
0        50      100 Miles

# AZTECS – WARRIORS OF THE SUN

THE AZTECS were a fierce tribe of warriors who settled in the Valley of Mexico in the 13th century AD. They fought endless wars with neighboring tribes, until they dominated most of Mesoamerica. Like the Mayas and Toltecs before them, they built spectacular cities. Their capital city at Tenochtitlán – where Mexico City now stands – lay on an island in Lake Texcoco. The island city was the center for around 200,000 Aztecs, or Mexica as they called themselves. Within the city wall there were palaces, pyramids, and temples where priests carried out terrible human sacrifices as part of a religious ritual to nourish the gods. The Aztecs believed they had to please their gods, or the world would come to an end.

The handle of this sacrificial knife is inlaid with precious turquoise and shell.

## AZTEC WARRIORS

The Aztecs were ruled by an emperor who was also in charge of the army. To keep their empire strong, all Aztec boys were trained to become warriors. When a boy reached the age of 10, his hair was cut, leaving a tuft of hair at the back. When he captured his first prisoner, the tuft of hair was cut. The best fighters became jaguar warriors and wore jaguar skins into battle, or they became eagle warriors and dressed with an eagle's head helmet.

Sacrifice was an important part of Aztec religion. Human hearts were offered to the Sun God.

Quetzalcoatl was a Toltec god who was also worshipped by the Aztecs.

**Tula**

**Tlacopán**
**Tenochtitlán**

**Texcoco**

LAKE TEXCOCO

The Emperor Montezuma was carried on a litter. Ordinary people were not allowed to look at him.

A Z T E C
E M P I R E

BALSAS

The Aztecs grew food on reclaimed swamp land known as chinampas.

Cacao beans were used to make a luxury drink, chocolate. The beans were so valuable that they were used as money.

Aztecs performed a daring ritual. Four men, tied by their ankles, swung out and around a pole.

**Mitla**

The Aztecs had no wheeled vehicles or strong pack animals. All trade goods were carried by porters.

Aztec warriors used a type of sling to hurl their spears at great speed.

P A C I F I C   O C E A N

## TRADE AND TREASURE

The Aztecs grew rich by collecting payments from conquered tribes. Cloth, corn, and luxury items were brought to Tenochtitlán from the defeated cities. The Aztecs also acquired goods by trade. Merchants called *pochteca* traveled all over the empire to bring back gold, silver, and tin, as well as precious stones of turquoise, jade, amethyst, and amber. Brightly colored feathers from exotic birds – quetzals and parrots – were also brought back to make cloaks and headdresses. Scribes kept detailed lists of the treasures taken from conquered cities.

G U L F   O F   M E X I C O

Spanish invaders, led by Hernán Cortés, landed at Cempoala in AD 1519.

**Cempoala**

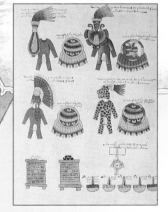

The main crop was corn, which farmers stored above ground in a special granary.

Scribes painted symbols onto bark which was folded into a book, called a *codex*. This page shows items taken as tribute.

TRADE ROUTE TO CENTRAL AMERICA

| 0 | 25 | 50 | 75 Kilometers |

| 0 | 25 | 50 Miles |

Temple of Tlaloc

Temple of Huitzilopochtli

**Ceremonial center of Tenochtitlán**

The round temple dedicated to the god, Quetzalcoatl

Temple of the Sun

The ball court

The Great Temple rose to a height of 200 ft (60 m).

Buildings were made of stone and were usually painted in bright colors.

Everyone had to remove their sandals before they entered the sacred enclosure to worship the gods.

Palaces and living quarters for priests and novices

## THE FLOATING CITY

The city of Tenochtitlán was built on a swamp in Lake Texcoco but was connected to the mainland by three wide causeways, or roads. At the heart of the city was a ceremonial center dominated by the Great Temple. At the top of a flight of steps there were two smaller temples – one dedicated to the rain god Tlaloc, the other to Huitzilopochtli, a Sun god and god of war. But in AD 1519, Spanish conquistadors (conquerors) invaded Mexico. Within two years they had destroyed the Aztec empire.

# INCAS – LORDS OF THE ANDES

THE EMPIRE OF THE INCAS was a land of great contrasts, dominated by the great mountain range of the snow-capped Andes. In this area of South America, several cultures had flourished – the Chavin, Moche, Nazca, and Chimú – but the greatest of all were the Incas. By about AD 1200, the Incas had developed from a small tribe living in the Andes into an organized society united under one ruler, called The Inca. From his capital at Cuzco, The Inca was worshiped as a living god – the son of the Sun. In AD 1438, the ruling Inca, Pachachuti Yupanqui, embarked on a program of conquest. Within a few years, the Incas had conquered a mighty empire that stretched 2,200 miles (3,500 km) along the Pacific coast of South America, covering much of modern Ecuador, Peru, Bolivia, and Chile.

### THE INCA

The Inca rulers were thought to be descended from the Sun god, Inti, which gave them absolute power over their subjects. The eighth Inca, Viracocha, took the title Sapa (Supreme) Inca, or emperor. The emperor dressed in clothes specially woven for him. In his ears he wore great golden discs. To keep the Sun's blood pure, the emperor married his sister. The sister-wife was called Coya, or empress. Although the emperor had many wives, only a son of the Coya could be the next emperor.

This gold and turquoise knife shows the figure of a richly dressed man. It was made by the Chimú people whose capital city was at Chan Chan.

The fortress at Cuzco, below, was made of neatly fitting stone blocks. During earthquakes they moved slightly, then fell back into place.

### CUZCO, CAPITAL CITY

Cuzco grew from a small village into a great capital city. The layout of the city was said to follow the shape of a puma, with the great fortress of Sacsahuamán forming the head. At the city center was the Haucaypata, or Holy Place. This was an open plaza where all the important ceremonies were held. There were also royal palaces and magnificent temples to the major gods. At the Temple of the Sun, there was a garden with life-size llamas, birds, and ears of corn, all made of gold and silver.

Machu Picchu was an important fortress city perched high in the Andes. It escaped the notice of the Spanish conquerors and was not discovered until 1911.

Women made a special drink called chicha by chewing corn into a pulp. They spat the pulp into warm water, which was then sieved into storage jars.

The fine wool of the alpaca was used to make warm clothing.

Young women were chosen to live in convents of the Sun where they spun and wove wool for the emperor's clothes.

A priest prepared a black llama for sacrifice to the gods.

Francisco Pizarro of Spain arrived in AD 1532, with an army of 200 men. Within a few years, his army had destroyed the mighty Inca Empire.

The Chimú people tried to invade the Inca empire. But an Inca prince, Yupanqui, destroyed their fortress and saved his people from invasion.

In November, the month of the dead, the mummified bodies of dead emperors were carried in a religious procession.

The Incas made bridges from rope, parts of which still survive, to cross deep chasms in the mountains.

### THE ROAD BUILDERS

The Incas built an impressive network of paved foot roads across their empire, overcoming incredible natural obstacles. They built stone bridges across rivers and suspension bridges made from twisted vines that spanned great chasms. Along the roads they built rest houses called tambos. Two runners were stationed at each tambo, ready to take messages at top speed to Cuzco from all across the empire. A team of runners could cover 150 miles (240 km) a day.

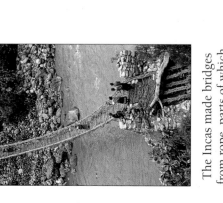

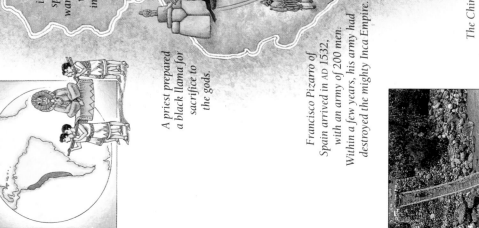

Quito

Tomebamba

Chan Chan

MARAÑON

Jauja

Pachácamac

INCA ROAD

Machu Picchu

Cuzco

Vilcashuamán

Nazca

INCA EMPIRE

A N D E S

Tiahuanaco

LAKE TITICACA

P A C I F I C

*Fishermen on the lakes used boats called balsas, made from bundles of reeds lashed together.*

*Masons used hammers to shape the stones for a city and then polished them with wet sand.*

*In the Andes, the farmers cut terraces into the mountainside to make fields. These fields were watered by an elaborate system of irrigation channels.*

## FATHER SUN AND MOTHER MOON

For the Incas, the Sun was the supreme god, and the most important temple was the Coricancha – the Temple of the Sun in Cuzco. But there were other gods and goddesses too, such as Mother Moon, the Thunder god, and Mother Earth. The Incas knew they had to serve their gods and treat them with respect or they would be punished with an illness or a bad harvest. There were rituals for every occasion when prayers and praises were said to the gods.

*Women often worked as healers, using plants, herbs, and roots as part of their medicine.*

*Llamas were the only pack animals available to the Incas.*

*A runner blew a conch shell to announce his arrival at a tambo. This warned the next runner that it was time to leave.*

LAKE POOPO

Tupiza

Pucara de Andagala

ANDES

ATACAMA DESERT

INCA ROAD

O C E A N

400 Kilometers
250 Miles
0 100 200 300
0 50 100 150 200 250

*Inca musicians played flutes, whistles, pan pipes, drums, tambourines, bells, and trumpets.*

## INCA SOCIETY

Inca society was extremely well organized. Everyone had their place and knew they would be cared for from cradle to grave. Orphans were provided for, while the sick, elderly, and disabled were fed and clothed from the royal storehouses. In return, everyone was expected to work hard. Suitable work was found for people, according to their rank, age, and ability. Inca rulers firmly believed that idle hands would get into mischief, so everyone had to be kept busy at all times.

*This photo shows a modern staging of the Feast of the Sun when Incas prayed for the Sun to rise in the sky the following summer.*

## TIED IN KNOTS

The Incas did not have any method of writing. But they did invent a way of recording things on a system of knotted cords, called *quipus*. Cords of various colors with single, double, or triple knots tied in them hung from a plain main cord. The number and position of the knots recorded such food supplies or number of llamas. A *quipu* could only be "read" by an official called a *quipucamayoc*.

*The waters along the coast were teeming with fish. Fresh-caught fish were carried by relays of runners to the emperor in Cuzco.*

*The Incas developed a system of keeping records by tying knots into colored ropes.*

## THE FARMING YEAR

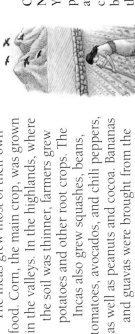

**August – September**
Men broke up the soil with a foot plow, while women sowed the seeds. People prayed to the Sun for a good harvest.

**October – November**
Young corn plants began to appear. Women cleared any blockages from the irrigation canals.

**December – January**
Weeding with hoes helped the young crops grow strong. A man and his wife often worked together.

The Incas grew most of their own food. Corn, the main crop, was grown in the valleys. In the highlands, where the soil was thinner, farmers grew potatoes and other root crops. The Incas also grew squashes, beans, tomatoes, avocados, and chili peppers, as well as peanuts and cocoa. Bananas and guavas were brought from the tropical lands east of the Andes. They also caught fish, birds, and wild animals in the countryside.

**June – July**
The main potato crop was picked and stored. When the harvest was in, the irrigation canals were cleaned and repaired.

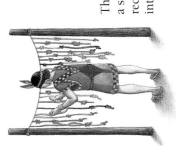

**April – May**
The corn was gathered and put into baskets, ready to store for the winter. Men, women, and children all turned out to help with the harvest.

**February – March**
The ripening corn had to be protected. People beat on drums to drive the birds away. Early potatoes and root crops were harvested.

# TIMECHART

THE TIMECHART on these pages summarizes the major events, battles, personalities, and inventions covered in this book. Entries have been organized in chronological order so you can trace the rise and fall of different civilizations, and also find out what was happening elsewhere in the world at the same time. Illustrations highlight some of the important rulers, architectural wonders, and events featured in the book.

*Building a step pyramid, Egypt*

*Bull leaping ceremony, Crete*

*Sargon of Akkad*

*Sea Peoples*

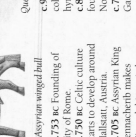
*Phoenician traders*

*Queen of Sheba visits Solomon*

*Great Bath at Mohenjo-Daro, Indus Valley*

*Bronze worker*

*Mycenaean death mask*

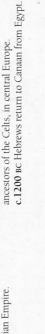
*New Kingdom pharaoh*

*King Hammurabi of Babylon records his laws*

*Stonehenge, England*

*City of Ugarit, Canaan*

*Sumerian scribes*

*Assyrian winged bull*

*Persian palace, Persepolis*

*Terra-cotta Nok head*

c.2500 BC Rise of Indus Valley civilization in India and Pakistan.
c.2500 BC Mesopotamians develop units for weights and measures.
c.2500 BC Central Asian people tame horses.
2500-2000 BC Spread of Beaker people throughout Northern Europe.
c.2350 BC Sargon unites cities of Akkad and then conquers Sumer.
2300 BC Earliest surviving map on baked clay tablet from Babylon.
c.2300 BC Pottery in use in Mexico and Guatemala.
c.2133-1633 BC Middle Kingdom in Egypt.

c.2100 BC The great ziggurat (temple tower) built at Ur in Sumer.
c.2000 BC Settlement of Pacific islands of Melanesia by emigrants from Indonesia.

c.3000 BC Agriculture in use in Mexico and Peru.
c.3000 BC Spread of megalith tombs across Europe.
2900 BC Port of Byblos founded in Phoenicia.
c.2750 BC Royal graves are dug at Ur in Sumer.
2686-2181 BC Old Kingdom in Egypt.
2650 BC Step pyramid built at Saqqara in Egypt.

c.2000-1450 BC Minoans build large palaces on Crete, including Knossos, Phaistos, and Mallia.
c.2000 BC Hittite states are set up in Anatolia.
c.2000 BC End of Sumer and Akkad.
c.2000 BC Skis are shown on Swedish rock carving.
c.2000 BC Shadow clocks in use by Egyptians.
c.2000 BC Sumer is invaded by Amorites.

c.3250 BC Cuneiform writing develops in Sumer.
c.3200 BC The wheel is invented in Sumer and used to make pottery and to move carts and chariots.
c.3000 BC Cochise hunter-gatherers are living in southwest North America.

c.2000 BC Start of the Bronze Age in the Near East.
1814-1754 BC First Assyrian Empire.
c.1800 BC First horse-drawn war chariot in the Middle East.

c.1800-900 BC Initial period in Peru. People settle in villages.
1792-1750 BC Reign of King Hammurabi of Babylon.

c.1028 BC Shang Dynasty in China overthrown by Chou Dynasty.
1020 BC Kingdom of Israel is established.
c.1000 BC Phoenicians produce simple alphabet, the basis of the alphabet we use today.
c.1000 BC In Australia, long-distance trade networks used for the exchange of ornaments and raw materials.
c.1000 BC Iron in use in Aegean and central Europe.
c.1000 BC Lapita settlers are established on Tonga and Samoa.

c.922 BC King Solomon dies; kingdom of Israel split into Judah and Israel.
c.911-612 BC New Assyrian Empire.
c.900 BC Rise of Chavin culture in Peru.
c.900 BC Etruscan civilization emerges in northern Italy.

c.900 BC The Rig Veda, a collection of 1,000 sacred hymns, is composed in India.
c.814 BC City of Carthage founded by Phoenicians in North Africa.
c.776 BC First Olympic Games held in Greece.

1200 BC Eastern Mediterranean invaded by the Sea Peoples.
c.1200-1000 BC Phoenicians rise to power.
c.1150 BC Destruction of Mycenaean civilization, start of Dark Ages in Greece.

c.1340 BC New Kingdom pharaoh, Tutankhamun, buried in the Valley of the Kings, Egypt.
c.1250 BC Legendary Trojan War fought between the Mycenaeans and the Trojans.
c.1200 BC Development of Urnfield culture, ancestors of the Celts, in central Europe.
c.1200 BC Hebrews return to Canaan from Egypt.

1450 BC Mycenaeans invade Crete.
c.1375-1047 BC Middle Assyrian Empire.

c.753 BC Founding of city of Rome.
c.750 BC Celtic culture starts to develop around Hallstatt, Austria.
c.705 BC Assyrian King Sennacherib makes Nineveh his capital.

671 BC Egypt conquered by Assyria.
c.612-539 BC Babylonian Empire dominates the Middle East.
c.600 BC Adena people farming and building burial mounds in North America.
c.563-483 BC Life of Siddhartha Gautama, the Buddha.
551-479 BC Life of Confucius.
c.550 BC Pythagoras develops his mathematical theorem.
549 BC Rise of Persian Empire under King Cyrus.

c.1500 BC Collapse of Indus Valley civilization.
c.1500 BC The Lapita people, ancestors of the Polynesians, expand outward from Indonesia.
c.1500 BC-AD 200 Olmec culture in Mexico.

c.1700 BC Canaanites use a new way of writing – an alphabet of 27 letters.
1650 BC Rise of the Hittite Kingdom in Anatolia.
1650 BC Rise of city-state of Mycenae in Greece.
c.1600 BC Building of Stonehenge in England is completed.
c.1595 BC Babylonia invaded by Kassites.
1567-1085 BC New Kingdom in Egypt.
c.1500-1028 BC Shang Dynasty in China.
c.1500 BC Deir el-Medina, the village for craftsmen who built the Egyptian royal tombs, is founded.
c.1500 BC Wet-rice agriculture begins in Korea.
c.1500 BC Cattle and goats domesticated in West Africa.

524-404 BC Egypt conquered and occupied by Persia.
c.500 BC Kingdom of Meroë, under kings of Napata, rises to power in northeast Africa.
c.500 BC Start of Nok culture in modern-day Nigeria.
c.500 BC First coins in China.
c.500 BC Celtic La Tène culture in Europe.
c.500 BC First copper smelting in West Africa.
c.490 BC Defeat of Persian King Darius at the Battle of Marathon.

73 BC Spartacus leads slave revolt against the Romans.
44 BC Julius Caesar appointed dictator of Rome for life; assassinated in the same year.
c.37-4 BC King Herod the Great rules Judea.
31 BC Cleopatra, Queen of Egypt, is defeated by Rome at the Battle of Actium.
30 BC Cleopatra and Mark Antony commit suicide. Egypt is now ruled by Rome.
27 BC Octavian becomes the first Roman Emperor; he takes the title of Augustus.
5 BC The first Shinto shrine is built at Ise in Japan.
c.4 BC-AD 29 Life of Jesus Christ in Judea.

*Roman soldiers*

*Dates change from BC to AD*

AD 1 Basketmaker people farming in southwest North America.
c.AD 24 Restoration and rise of Han Dynasty in China.
AD 43 Romans invade and conquer Britain.
c.AD 50 Kushan Empire established in northern India.

c.AD 793 Vikings begin raiding Europe.
AD 794-1185 Heian Period in Japan. New capital city at Heian-kyo (Kyoto).
c.AD 800 Ghana rises to prominence in West Africa.
c.AD 800 Aboriginal culture well-established in Australia.
AD 800-1800 Kingdom of Kanem-Borno in West Africa.
AD 868 Diamond Sutra, earliest known book, printed in China.
AD 900 Maya start their emigration into Yucatan. Rise of Toltecs in Mexico.
c.AD 900 Civilization of Igbo Ukwu in West Africa.
AD 907 Start of Mongol expansion in Inner Mongolia and northern China.
AD 920 Golden Age of Ghana begins.

*Aboriginal storytelling*

*Polynesian boats*

c.AD 950 Polynesians reach New Zealand.
AD 982 Vikings under Erik the Red settle in Greenland.
AD 998-1038 Stephen I (St. Stephen) becomes first king of Hungary.
c.AD 1000 Gunpowder in use in China.
AD 1016 Cnut, Danish king, becomes king of England.

---

c.480 BC Greek naval victory at Salamis.
431-404 BC Peloponnesian War; Athens is defeated by Sparta.
429 BC Pericles, who organized the rebuilding of the Parthenon in Athens, dies of plague.
403-221 BC Period of warring states in China.

*Great Wall of China*

221-210 BC First empire in China, ruled by Emperor Ch'in.
c.217 BC Hannibal, a Carthaginian general, defeats the Romans at Trasimeno.
c.200 BC Nazca people living in southern Peru.
c.300 BC Spread of Yayoi culture in Japan.
285 BC First known lighthouse built at Pharos, Egypt.
c.272-231 BC King Asoka rules Mauryan Empire in India.
c.250 BC Rise of Maya civilization in Central America.

168 BC Jewish revolt against the Seleucid kings led by Judas Maccabeus, a village priest from near Jerusalem.
c.100 BC Hohokam people living in southeast North America.

*Writing on paper, China*

AD 79 Mount Vesuvius erupts and destroys Pompeii.
AD 100 Rise of Axum, ancient kingdom of Ethiopia in north Africa.
c.AD 100 Paper is invented in China.
c.AD 100 Steam engine designed by Hero of Alexandria, Egypt.

*Queen Boudicca, Britain*

AD 60 Queen Boudicca leads revolt against Romans in Britain.
AD 70-80 Colosseum built in the center of Rome.
AD 74 Jewish stronghold of Masada is destroyed by Romans at the end of the Jewish revolt.

*Palace at Ch'ang'an, China*

AD 710-794 Nara Period in Japan.
AD 745 First newspaper printed in China.
AD 750 In India, three empires at war with each other.
AD 756 Uprising in Ch'ang'an, capital city of the T'ang Dynasty, at start of Silk Road in China.
AD 768-814 Rule of Charlemagne, founder of the Frankish Empire in Europe.

*Dancers at Angkor Wat*

AD 1050 Height of Khmer kingdom in Southeast Asia.
AD 1066 William of Normandy becomes king of England after Battle of Hastings.
AD 1096 First Crusade to the Holy Land to win it back from the Muslims. Jerusalem taken.
c.AD 1100 Rise of kingdom of Ife in modern-day Nigeria.

---

*The Parthenon, Athens*

c.400 BC The Nabataeans carve their capital city of Petra from rock.
c.399 BC Greek philosopher Socrates is put to death while in prison.

AD 285 Diocletian co-rules the Roman Empire with Maximian.
c.AD 300 Yamato government is established in Japan.
AD 300-200 Hopewell people replace the Adena culture in Ohio.
AD 320 Gupta Dynasty founded in India.
AD 395 Roman Empire divided, with Western Empire based in Rome and Eastern Empire based in Constantinople.
AD 400 People from Tonga and Samoa colonize Polynesian islands of the Pacific.
AD 400 Start of settlement of city of Jenne-jeno on River Niger.
AD 410 Visigoths, a Germanic race, sack Rome.
AD 432 St. Patrick converts Ireland to Christianity.
AD 449 onward: Angles, Saxons, and Jutes invade England.

*War elephants of King Asoka*

c.387 BC Celtic Gauls invade the city of Rome.
356-323 BC Life of Alexander the Great of Greece.

*Queen of Meroë*

c.AD 122 Romans build Hadrian's Wall as northern boundary of their empire in Britain.
c.AD 150 Ptolemy of Greece produces map of the known world.
AD 200-600 Moche people flourish in Peru.
AD 220 Fall of Han Dynasty in China.
c.AD 250 Kingdom of Meroë starts to decline.

*Mica hand, Hopewell*

*Iron smelting, Africa*

AD 451 Attila and the Huns invade Gaul.
AD 476 Western Roman Empire comes to an end.
c.AD 500 Bantu ironworkers in southern Africa.

*Maya temple*

AD 618-907 T'ang Dynasty in China.
c.AD 675 Maya culture flourishes in Central America.
AD 700-1000 Hohokam people at the height of their development in North America.

*March to Mecca*

AD 531 Axum in northern Africa is converted to Christianity.
AD 571-632 Life of Mohammed, founder of Islam.
AD 610 Eastern Roman Empire becomes known as the Byzantine Empire.

*Samurai warrior*

AD 1167-1227 Life of Genghis Khan, founder of Mongol Empire and Khan dynasty.
AD 1185-1333 Kamakura period in Japan and rise of samurai.
AD 1187 Muslim leader Saladin wins back Jerusalem.
AD 1215 Signing of Magna Carta by King John of England.

*Aztec Emperor Montezuma*

AD 1254-1324 Life of Marco Polo, Venetian traveler.
AD 1337-1453 Hundred Years' War fought between France and England.
c.AD 1348-1352 Black Death (bubonic plague) kills one-third of the population of Europe.
AD 1368 Foundation of Ming Dynasty in China.
AD 1369-1405 Tamerlane rules the Mongols.
AD 1431 Joan of Arc burned at the stake in France.
AD 1436-1464 Rule of Aztec Emperor Montezuma I.

*Inca builders at Cuzco*

AD 1438 Inca Empire at its height in Peru.
AD 1452-1519 Life of Leonardo da Vinci, Italian artist.
AD 1453 Ottomans capture Constantinople.
AD 1462 Ivan III, the Great, founds Russian Empire.
AD 1464 Sunni Ali rules Songhay people in West Africa.
AD 1478 Ferdinand and Isabella conquer the last Muslim stronghold in Spain.
AD 1492 Christopher Columbus reaches the West Indies.
AD 1501 Italian Amerigo Vespucci (who gave his name to the American continents) explores the coast of Brazil.

# INDEX

## A

Aboriginals, 7, 52, 63
Acropolis, 34, 35
Actium, Battle of, 39, 63
Adena people, 6, 50, 62
Africa ,24, 44-45
Akkad, 11, 28, 62
Alexander the Great, 25, 32, 33, 36-37, 46, 63
alphabet, see writing
Amorites, 7, 10, 62
Amun, 14
Anasazi, 51
Angkor Wat, 57, 63
ankh, 14
Antigonus, 36
Arabia/Arabs, 7, 42-43, 45
archaeologists, 8, 9, 10, 20, 57
architecture, Greek, 37
armies,
  Assyrian, 28, 29;
  Aztec, 59;
  Babylonian, 27;
  Chinese, 49, 54;
  Egyptian, 14, 15;
  Greek, 34, 46;
  Persian, 32;
  Roman, 7, 30, 31, 39;
  Spartan, 35;
  Sumerian, 10
Artemis, 36
Ashur, 28
Asoka, King, 46, 47, 63
Assyria, 7, 26, 28-29, 62
Athene, 34, 35, 36
Athens, 34, 35, 63
Augustus, 38, 63
Australia, 52, 62, 63
Axum, 7, 43, 44, 45, 63
Aztecs, 6, 59, 63

## B

Babylon/Babylonia, 7, 26-27, 28, 32, 62
Bantu-speakers, 7, 44, 45, 63
barbarians, 39
barrows, 18
bedouin, 42, 43
Benin, 44, 45
boats, 12, 53; see also dhows, ships
Boudicca, Queen, 30, 63
bronze, 11, 17, 18, 19
Bronze Age, 4, 18, 62
Buddha/Buddhism, 46, 47, 54, 55, 56, 57, 63
burial, 15, 20, 49; see also barrows, tombs

## C

Cairo, 44
Cambyses, King, 32
Canaan, 7, 22, 24, 62
Carthage, 24, 44, 62
caste system, 47
Celts, 6, 30-31, 62
Ceylon, 47
Chaldeans, 26, 27
Chams, 57
Ch'angan, 54, 63
chariots, 11, 15, 33
Chichén Itzá, 58
Chimu people, 60

Ch'in, 7, 48
Ch'in Shi Huang Ti, Emperor, 48, 63
China, 48-49, 54-55, 62, 63
Christianity, 39, 45, 63
city states,
  Canaanite, 22;
  Greek, 7, 34, 35
civilizations, 4; map of, 6-7
Cleopatra, Queen, 39, 63
clothing,
  Celtic, 30;
  Egyptian, 13;
  European, 19;
  Greek, 35;
  Roman, 40
codex, 59
Colosseum, Rome, 8, 41, 63
Confucius/Confucianism, 55, 62
copper, 10, 17, 18, 19, 25, 42
Cortes, Hernan, 59
Crete, 20, 21, 62
Cush, 44,
Cuzco, 60, 61, 63
Cyrus, King, 26, 27, 32, 33, 62

## D

Darius, King, 25, 32, 33, 35, 62
dating systems, 4;
  techniques, 8, 9
Delphi, 31, 34
democracy, 34
dhows, 43
Diamond Sutra, 54, 63
Dreamtime ancestors, 52
druids, 31

## E, F

East African people, 7, 45
Easter Island, 53
Edo, 45
Edom, 23, 42
Egypt/Egyptians, 4, 7, 9, 12-13, 14-15, 32, 36, 62
Elam/Elamites, 7, 11
Ephesus, 4, 34
Eskimos, see Inuit
Euphrates River, 10, 11
Europe, 18-19, 20, 62
Ewuare the Great, 45
Ezana, King, 45
farmers/farming, 4, 6, 10, 12, 18, 23, 29, 61
Fertile Crescent, 6, 7
flooding of the Nile, 12, 13
Fujiwara clan, 56

## G

Galli tribe/Galatia, 7, 31
Ganges River, 47
Gaugamela, Battle of, 36
Gaul, 30, 38, 63
Gautama, Siddhartha, 46, 62
Gempei War, 56
Germani tribes, 7, 30
Ghana, 6, 44, 45, 63
gladiators, 41
gods/goddesses,
  Arabian, 42;
  Babylonian, 27;
  Canaanite, 22;
  Celtic, 31;
  Egyptian, 14;
  Greek, 36;
  Inca, 60, 61;
  Indus Valley, 17;
  Minoan, 20, 21;

Mycenaean, 21;
Polynesian, 53;
Roman, 39;
Sumerian, 10, 11
Granicus, Battle of, 36
Great Wall of China, 4, 48, 49
Great Zimbabwe, 44, 45
Greece, 7, 20, 21, 31, 33, 34-35, 36-37, 63
Gutian tribes, 11

## H

Hadrian, Emperor, 38, 63
Hallstatt culture, 30, 31, 62
Hammurabi, King, 26, 62
Hanging Gardens of Babylon, 26, 27
Hannibal, 38, 63
Harappa, 16
Hatshepsut, Queen, 14
Hebrew tribes, 7, 23, 62
Heian Period, Japan, 56, 63
Herodotus, 35
hieroglyphics, 8, 15
Hinduism, 47, 57
Hittites, 7, 21, 22, 26, 62
Hohokam culture, 51, 63
Hopewell people, 6, 50, 51, 63
hoplites, 25
Horus, 14
housing, 8;
  African, 45;
  Celtic, 31;
  Egyptian, 12;
  Greek, 37;
  Hebrew, 23;
  Indus Valley, 16;
  Japanese, 56;
  Roman, 39, 40-41
Hsiung Nu tribes, 48
Hsuan Tsang, 54
Huns, 39, 48, 63
Hydaspes River, Battle of, 36, 37
Hyksos, 15, 22

## I

Ibn Battuta, 44
Iceni tribe, 30
Igloos, 50, 51
Incas, 6, 60-61, 63
India, 16-17, 46-47, 63
Indo-Aryans, 16, 17
Indus Valley, 7, 16-17, 62
Inuit, 6, 50, 51
Ionia, 32, 33, 35
iron, 30, 44, 45, 48
Iron Age, 4, 30
Iroquois, 51
Ishtar Gate, 26, 27
Islam, 42, 43, 45
Israel, 23, 62
Issus, Battle of, 36

## J

Jainism, 47
Japan, 7, 56, 63
Jayavarman II, King, 57
Jayavarman VII, King, 57
Jenne, 44
Jericho, 22
Jerusalem, 23, 26, 27, 63
Jesus Christ, 39, 63
Jews, 23, 32
Jimmu Tenno, 56
Judah/Judea, 23, 27, 39, 62
Julius Caesar, 30, 38, 63

## K, L

Kaaba, 42
Kassites, 7, 26, 27, 62
Khmer Kingdom, 7, 57, 63
Khoikhoi, 45
Kilwa, Sultan of, 45
Knossos, 20, 62
Kyoto, 56
La Tène culture, 30, 62
Lalibela, King, 44
Lao-tze, 55
lugal, 10
Lydia, 32

## M

Maccabees, Judas, 23, 63
Macedonia, 34, 36
Machu Picchu, 60
Magadha, 46
Mahabharata, 47
Makah people, 6, 50
Mali, 44, 45
Maoris, 7, 53
maps/mapmakers, 5
Marathon, Battle of, 32, 35, 62
Marduk, 26, 27
Ma'rib, 42, 43
Mark Antony, 39, 63
Masada, 23, 63
Massagetae, 7, 33
mastabas, 15
Maurya, Chandragupta, 46
Mauryan Empire, 7, 46-47, 63
Maya, 6, 58, 63
Mecca, 42, 43, 63
Medes, 7, 28, 32
Media, 32
Medina, 42, 43
Meroë, 7, 44, 62, 63
Mesopotamia, 10, 11, 62
Minamoto Yoritomo, 56
Minoans, 7, 20-21, 63
Minotaur, 21
Mississippians, 6, 51
Mitanni, 7, 22
Mohenjo-Daro, 16, 62
money, 34, 48, 59, 62
monument builders, 6, 18-19
mother goddess,
  European, 19;
  Indus Valley, 17
mound builders, North
  American, 50, 51
mummification, 9, 15
Muslims, 42, 44, 45
Mycenaeans, 7, 20-21, 62

## N, O

Nabataeans, 42, 63
Nabonidus, King, 26, 27
Nabopolassar, King, 26, 27
Nara, 56, 63
Native Americans, 6, 50, 51
Nebuchadnezzar, King, 26, 27
Necho II, Pharaoh, 25
Nero, Emperor, 43
New Zealand, 53, 63
Nile River, 4, 12-13, 14, 15
Nineveh, 28, 29
Nok culture, 7, 44, 45, 62
nomads, 22, 42
North America, 50-51
Nubia, 7, 13, 44
Octavian, Emperor, 38, 39, 63
Ojibwa people, 51

oligarchy, 34
Olmecs, 6, 58, 62
Olympic Games, 34, 37, 62

## P, Q

Pachachuti Yupanqui, 60
Pacific Ocean islands, 53
palaces,
  African 44, 45;
  Arabian 44;
  Assyrian 28, 29;
  Babylonian 27;
  Chinese 54;
  Minoan 20, 21;
  Persian 32, 33;
  Phoenician 25
Palenque, 8, 58
Palmyra, 43
paper, 15, 54, 55, 63
Pataliputra, 46, 47
Peleset, 23
Pergamum, 31
Pericles, 34, 63
Persepolis, 32, 33
Persia, 7, 32-33, 35, 36, 37, 62
Persian Wars, 35
Petra, 42, 63
pharaohs, 14, 15, 62
Philistines, 23
philosophers, Greek, 37
Phoenicians, 7, 24-25, 62
Pizarro, Francisco, 60
Plains tribes, 50, 51
Plataea, Battle of, 34, 35
plow, 4, 11
Polynesia/Polynesians, 6, 53, 63
Poseidon, 36
pottery, 8, 10, 17, 19, 21, 25, 34, 50, 51, 62
preservation of ancient
  remains, 9
printing, 54, 55
Ptolemy, 36, 63
Pueblo people, 6, 50, 51
Punic Wars, 24, 39
pyramids, 14, 15, 62
Pythagoras, 37, 62
quipus, 61

## R

radiocarbon dating, 9
religion, see gods/goddesses and
  individual religions
republic, 38
Rig Veda, 47, 62
rivers, development of
  civilizations beside, 6
roads, 32, 33, 38, 39, 60, 61
Roman Empire, 5, 7, 38-39, 63
Romans, 23, 24, 30
Rome, 31, 40-41, 62
Rosetta Stone, 8
Roxane, 36, 37

## S

Sahara Desert, 4, 44
Salamis, Battle of, 35
Samoa, 53, 62, 63
Samurai, 56
Sanskrit, 46
Sappho, 35
Sargon, King, 11, 62
satrapies, 32, 33
scribes, 11, 59
Scythians, 7, 32
Sea Peoples, 7, 23, 24, 62
Seleucus, 36, 46

Sennacherib, King, 28, 62
Senusret III, Pharaoh, 14
shaduf, 13
Shinto, 56
ships,
  Greek, 35;
  Phoenician, 24, 25;
  see also boats, dhows
shoguns, 56
Shona Empire, 7, 45
shrines, 21, 31
Siam, 7, 57
Silk Road, 54, 55, 63
Solomon, King, 23, 62
Songhay, 44, 45, 63
Spartans, 34, 35
Stone Age, 4
Stonehenge, 18, 62
Sumer, 7, 10-11, 28, 62
Susa, 32

## T

Tahiti Islands, 53
T'ang, 7, 54
T'ang T'ai-tsung, Emperor, 54
Taoism, 55
temples, 8;
  Aztec, 59;
  Canaanite, 22;
  Egyptian, 14;
  Greek, 35, 37;
  Hebrew, 23;
  Inca, 60, 61;
  Sumerian, 10
Tenochtitlán, 59
Thermopylae, Battle of, 35
Tiglath-pileser III, King, 29
Tigris River, 10, 28
tin, 17, 18, 19
tombs,
  Chinese, 49;
  Egyptian, 14, 15;
  Sumerian, 10;
  see also barrows, burial
Tonga, 53, 62, 63
Trojan War, 21, 62
Troy, 21

## U, V

Ugarit, 22
Ur, 10, 11, 62
Urartu, 29
Ur-Nammu, King, 10, 11
Urnfield culture, 18, 19, 62
Veneti tribe, 30
Vikings, 51, 63

## W, X, Y, Z

wheel, 10, 17, 62
writing, 8;
  Canaanite, 22, 62;
  Chinese, 48;
  Egyptian, 8, 12, 15;
  Japanese, 56;
  Maya, 58;
  Meroitic, 44;
  Minoan, 21;
  Phoenician, 24, 62;
  Sumerian, 11, 62
written records, 8
Wu, Empress, 54, 55
Xerxes, King, 32, 33, 35
Yayoi culture, 56, 63
Zenobia, Queen, 43
Zeus, 34, 36
ziggurats, 10, 26, 27, 62
Zoroaster/Zoroastrianism, 33

## ACKNOWLEDGMENTS

Dorling Kindersley would like to thank the following:
Lynn Bresler for help with the Timechart; Peter Bull
and Richard Ward for additional artwork; Michelle de
Larrabeiti for research; Hussain Mohamed for design
assistance.

**Map consultant** Roger Bullen

**Picture research** Diana Morris

**Locator globes** John Woodcock

**Index** Lynn Bresler

### Picture Credits
Abbreviations/key: r=right, l=left, t=top, c=center, b=below

Ancient Art & Architecture Collection: 31cr, 35c, 48c, 55tr, 55br.
Bodleian Library, Oxford: 5br.
Bridgeman Art Library: 14b British Museum; 37bc Christies, London; 40t Getty Museum, Malibu; 41c Bonhams, London.
Trustees of the British Library, India Office Library: 54cr.
Trustees of the British Museum: 4bl, 8tr, 8c, 9l, 10bl, 10br, 14c, 19br, 21br, 22b, 24tr, 25cr, 26cr, 28c, 28bl, 28bc, 30bc, 31c, 32b, 33tl, 33c, 34c, 56c, 59tr.
J.Allan Cash: 39t.
Lester Cheeseman: 46cl.
Chip Clark 1993: 9bl.
C. M. Dixon, Photoresources: 17c, 20, 46bl.
E.T. Archive: 48t Bibliothèque Nationale, Paris.
Mary Evans Picture Library: 35t, 37tl, 38b, 50cl.

Chris Fairclough: 13tl.
Werner Forman Archive: 15tr; 44tr Sudan Museum, Khartoum; 45c Entwistle Gallery, London; 45bl British Museum; 51b Glenbow Museum, Calgary; 53b Auckland Institute.
Robert Harding Picture Library: 4c, 4br, 6bl, 14cr; 14bc Louvre; 15br; 29cl British Museum; 37cr, 38t, 40b; 42bcr Chester Beatty Library, Dublin; 43cr Jack Jackson; 46br, 49cr, 49bc, 49br, 52bl, 54cl, 57tr; 60cb Rob Frerck; 61tl.
Michael Holford: 8br; 10c, 11tr, 13c, 14tl British Museum; 17tr Musée Guimet; 24bl, 36cl, 42c, 45br British Museum; 47tr, 53cr; 57bl Musée Guimet; 58cl; 58cr British Museum; 60c.
Hutchison Picture Library: 12tr Liba Taylor; 13tl Chris Parker; 17b, 47bl, 51cr, 60tr; 60cl H.R.Dorig.
Images Colour Library/Douglas Baglin: 52tr.
The Israel Museum: 22cl, 22cr.

Erich Lessing Archive: 26bl, 27.
John Marr: 46cr.
McQuitty International Collection: 16t, 17cr.
Nationalmuseet, Denmark/Kit Weiss: 19tr.
Ohio Historical Society, Columbus/photographer Dirk Bakker: 50b.
R.M.N. Paris: 26c Louvre; 30cl St.Germain-en-Laye; 41b Louvre/Chuzeville.
Royal Pavilion, Art Gallery & Museums, Brighton: 19cr.
St. Louis Museum of Science & Natural History/photographer Dirk Bakker: 51tr.
Scala: 7bl Vatican Museums; 7cl; 21c National Museum, Athens; 21bc Heraklion Museum; 24 El Prado; 33tr National Museum, Naples; 37tr, 41t.
Science Photo Library: Cambridge University Collection of Air Photographs 9br; Bruce Iverson 9bc.
Spectrum Colour Library: 23t.
Zefa: 12br, 13c, 29cr, 38c, 42bc,42bcl Havlicek; 57br.